MW01289766

SIGNS ALONG THE PATH
A Guide to an Inspired Life

Remember, you are the Avatar!

John Davis and Holly Matson

Copyright 2010 by John Davis

Go create, my sister!

Holly

JOHN OF PENIEL

Production Team
John Davis, author
Holly Matson, author and project manager
Kelly Cochran, cover design

With thanks to MaryAnn Rimes for editing and proofreading.

Table of Contents

Foreword

As I walked down the pathway of my life, I found myself ever on a spiritual quest. It began in a very structured fundamental religion way and changed to become a very present moment experience. My teachers have been many. They have come from all walks of life. Some you might not have recognized as teachers if you saw them on the path. Each was enlightening and eye opening for me as I met them and came to know the message they brought to me along the path. Each message or sign I encountered built upon the last in a synchronistic perfection that allowed me to see its meaning. When I recognized each sign it was mind blowing and I was propelled forward towards the next.

After a time I began to realize that although I had seen the signs and heard the messages, I did not take note of the direction the signs pointed. The words were different but the arrows all pointed in the same direction. As I began to walk the path following the direction the signs pointed, they led me back to myself.

Throughout time humanity has had many teachers both modern and ancient. Each of these teachers brought many spiritual truths. Each came as a signpost for humanity to show us our divinity and our place in creation. As I walked my personal path, I began to journal my experiences. My hope was to share the signs along my path as a means for others to follow to the same destination. All the teachers led you to you. Your power is unequaled in the universe and your place in creation is to be a co-creator with the source of all that is.

The teachings are not new. They are timeless truths. They lead you home to yourself. Some will be funny. Some will be poignant, but all are intended to lead you home. I hope you enjoy this journey as we walk side by side along your path.

My thanks to my dear friend Holly for first being my friend, and second for compiling this book. I know her intention, as well as mine, is to help as many people find their divinity within as we can.

Choose a blessed life, after all if you're the creator, choosing anything else would just be silly.

~ **John Davis**

Introduction

Back in the early part of the twentieth century, one of the best-known advertising campaigns of the United States began – Burma Shave signs. If you are not aware of this American icon, the promotion was the placement of a sequence of signposts along the road, usually five or six, that each contained a portion of a message. The last would show the name of the product (Burma Shave) or the punchline of a joke. Here's one for example: "No matter the price . . . no matter how new . . . the best safety device. . . in your car is you . . . Burma Shave."

Now, as we're traveling the road of life, we drive along just going wherever the road takes us, paying little attention to the view, with no clear goal in mind. Sometimes we'll get lost, or we'll get mad at the wrong turns or confusing traffic signals. We create most of our journey by drifting unconsciously along the road.

Then there are those of us who go through life based on what others tell us which way we *should* go, because that's the way they went. *Should* is a nasty word that tells you that you are wrong. Are you wrong for preferring blue to red? Cool temperatures to summer heat? Mountain scenery to flatlands? Of course not! And certainly you are not wrong for making choices in your life that may differ from the choices of those around you. Only you can make those decisions.

You can decide to live your life by a different method, one taken by many spiritually evolving people: creating the journey consciously, by following your own internal maps and GPS devices, and by paying attention to signposts along the way. Sometimes these signs contain messages of importance, and sometimes they're simply encouragement, but they are always sequential, just like the Burma Shave signs. When we learn that the guidance exists and learn to watch for it, we find that by taking inspired action based on the signs (like choosing to do what the message suggests), our lives of conscious creation seem so much easier and more enjoyable.

So, now you're traveling down your road of life fully aware and creating consciously by making your own decisions. You choose to ignore the detour signs and end up at a dead end – your choice had consequences, but you can now choose differently based on the consequence, and turn around. Or you may get distracted by something on the road and miss the last directional sign, the punchline to the message, and realize you've taken a wrong turn. When you become aware of these "mis-takes" then you can consciously create a new experience and go back and try a different way. You learn through these events that following guidance that feels right for you leads to a life that feels fulfilling.

This book is intended to be a sequence of signposts, like those Burma Shave signs of old. It reveals options you may not have thought of, concepts that may be new to you. One of the great new-age teachers, Abraham (www.abraham-hicks.com), tells us that the knowing of what you do not want leads to the knowing of what you do want. The contrast between the two can be bridged by the awareness of your thoughts, which leads to a change in your feelings, which leads to a change in your beliefs, until at last you are hearing the music of your ideal life. Each chapter of this book discusses a topic intended to help you become aware of your thoughts, feelings and beliefs – just as those road signs bring you to the final goal.

Most spiritual teachers say that there are only two true states of being: love and fear. One is joyful, positive, loving; the other is sad, afraid, negative and sometimes hateful. I believe that God intended for his children to live joyfully, abundantly, and lovingly. Now if we truly understand the foundation of John Davis's teaching -

that God does not want followers, he wants creators - then it is a natural next step to ask how we can create joyfully, positively and lovingly.

Our intent is to show you how truly simple it is to re-program your spiritual GPS, to follow new signs and to re-start your life from this very moment. Savor the creation and enjoy the view: As John says, the message is simple – **be love**!

~ **Holly Matson**

Chapter 1. Manifestation and Creation

We in the human condition often feel that things "happen" to us, things out of our control. "Why does this always happen to me?" "See, I knew this would happen." "I hate being stuck in this job." "I can't ever get ahead." "Why am I always sick?" Far from being the victims, observers and participants of our lives, science is now proving that instead, we are the creators of them.   Quantum physicists have shown that the mere act of observing an atom changes its characteristics. The implications are tremendous. John discusses the importance of awareness, along with correct thought and feeling, to take charge of our own condition.   Learn the importance of changing your life to one that pleases and empowers you. Reprogram your GPS to the joyful scenic route! ~ HM

Another Moment

"Life belongs to the living, and he who lives must be prepared for changes".
~Johann Wolfgang von Goethe

This year my life has been hectic to say the least. I have been working several jobs at once to try and catch up. I find myself falling back onto things that have supported me in the past. I also find myself unsatisfied by the experience. I had yet again a moment of clarity when I spoke to the Ohio Metaphysical Society. The speech yielded the group's highest attendance, more   potential speeches, and most importantly many healings. I return to my life as is and find that the clarity of the path ahead makes my present location on the path less desirable. It is   precisely at these moments, the moments of greatest dissatisfaction, that you can make giant leaps in your life.

"Everyone who's serious about what they're doing must be in constant motion forward". ~Ed O'Brien

I look ahead and see the future, the model I am bringing to my life. I focus on it and realize that for that reality to be this reality I must let go of present conditions. We sometimes build velvet cages. We are comfortable in them, we think of them as home and yet we cannot fly and be free. Though they are velvety and comfortable, they are still cages. Eventually you want to fly to something new.

Recognize your cage as a cage. Cages are not in motion. Cages sit stagnant. Cages do not let your wings stretch or your dreams fly. Pick the lock, jump into the air and fly. The hands of God will lift you and you will soar to the greatest heights. Do what fills you and the Universe will support you.

"Be like the bird that, passing on her flight awhile on boughs too slight, feels them give way beneath her, and yet sings, knowing that she hath wings".
~Victor Hugo

Hope

As I have said in an earlier blog, I am fascinated by words. They are how we express ourselves, communicate, and manifest. I often say that we need to be careful what we ask for because the universe starts creating as soon as we ask or declare. When we declare with words like 'need' or 'want' God gives us need or want. The interesting thing is that words like 'hope' can slow our manifestation process. When we 'hope" for something it means it is in a future moment and not the present. We can only receive in the present so focusing on the future timeline can actually keep your dreams ahead of you as opposed to coming to fruition. Words like 'I AM' are present timeline which is why when we ask God/ Universe we should always ask in the present tense so we can receive it here. Besides God's name according to Moses is I AM. Just a thought.

"What I am looking for is not out there, it is in me". ~Helen Keller

Thoughts

"Man is made by his belief. As he believes, so he is" --The Bhagavad Gita

Thoughts become things. This statement is true and has been so since the dawn of consciousness. Thought is the beginning of creation. Declaration of thought is the stone thrown in the pond that creates the ripples of potential. Choice is focused thought put into action. Gratitude is faith, which brings the culmination of thought.

"All that we are is the result of what we have thought. If a man speaks or acts with an evil thought, pain follows him. If a man speaks or acts with a pure thought, happiness follows him, like a shadow that never leaves him".
–Buddha

Thoughts are prayers. The pond of potential is God/ Universe/ Goddess. It is an unlimited pond with unlimited resources and unlimited potentials. The limits placed upon it are ours. Our faith in what CAN be achieved marks the limits of our faith. The mark of your past faith is where you stand now. The experience you want is just a thought away.

As we live in residuals, the continuing to choose a thought until it is in our hands is the manifestation process. Be grateful first, choose the outcome, declare with," I AM" and receive your desires.

"The good man brings good things out of the good stored up in his heart, and the evil man brings evil things out of the evil stored up in his heart. For out of the overflow of his heart his mouth speaks." -- Jeshua

Potential

"Consult not your fears but your hopes and your dreams. Think not about your frustrations, but about your unfulfilled potential. Concern yourself not with what you tried and failed in, but with what it is still possible for you to do." ~Pope John XXIII

"What you think you become." "Greater works than I have done you will do." "We are the culmination of our thoughts." "With faith as small as a mustard seed you may ask a mountain to move and it will move." These are the words of the Avatars of old. Each reached a place to be admired. Each reached the heights of his potential. Each told us it is our potential. Each accepted his personal role in divinity and affected the world around him. When they walked among us they each told us we are divine and all we have to do is take our place.

It's the "taking" where we get confused. To "take a place" is an interesting concept. We can take a place in a line or we can take the place of leader. What each Avatar asked of us was to take the role of leader in our own lives. It seems selfish to be sure. It is, however, through our own personal enlightenment that we can enlighten those around us. Each of the Avatars led by example. They lived the life of our potential. They asked us to follow their lead, so we could lead ourselves. As we reach the heights of our potential they ask us to lead those behind us so they can lead those behind them.

The true peacemakers of the world would love it if the world thought like they do. So they show another way in hopes that it would catch on and change the world. Each Avatar would love it if the world thought like they do, so they showed another way, each hoping to change the world to reach its fullest potential.

"Be the change you want to see in the world"~ Mahatma Gandhi

Live a loving life, give love, receive love, expect nothing less. You are Love. God is Love. Accept your role as a part of something

4

greater and resonate with it and feel lighter. Become En-Lightened. Resonate with the vibrational song of love and listen as the world harmonizes with you. Watch as the lights come up on a perfect life. Witness the standing ovation of the universe and come in harmony with your potential. There is NOTHING to fear. It is only you and your potential without limits.

"Your range of available choices - right now - is limitless". ~Frederick C. Frieseke

My Prayer Formula

"Develop an attitude of gratitude, and give thanks for everything that happens to you, knowing that every step forward is a step toward achieving something bigger and better than your current situation." ~Brian Tracy

Over the years I have come to see many positive results from prayer. I slowly refined the way I pray. I first realized that to see results of a prayer, it has to be a prayer in the present moment. Next I have to be grateful for the result I have already achieved. The Bible says whatsoever we wish, ask in God's name. Moses climbed a mountain and talked to God in the form of a burning bush. At the end of that conversation Moses asked God his name. God said "I AM." Then I have to declare it in the present moment.

So I start my prayer formula with gratitude:

Thank you God

I then move to the object of my prayer:

For the____ (whatever I am asking for)

I move on to God's Name:

I AM

Next is the action step:

receiving,

Now to end in the present moment:

Amen

The word Amen when translated means "so be it," not "so it will be" or "so it was."

Thank you God for the healing I AM receiving Amen.

The next step is faith. I have to believe that it is true and act accordingly. In using this formula over the years I have seen it work every time. Give it a try and watch the miracles happen.

"I Am that I Am" ~Exodus

You Are The Avatar

"Greater works than I have done you will do." "It is your faith that heals you." "You are the children of God." Each of these statements from an Avatar of the past tells us that we are as he was and is. We each set the limits of our potential and since we set the limits then we are truly limitless. The Source of all that is - God, Universal Consciousness, mother earth, whatever you call it - creates whatever we ask of it. Our unconscious creations have brought us to where we are at this moment in time.

The Avatar takes the role by stepping into conscious creation with the Source. The "greater works" are your conscious creations that will indeed alter humanity. I use the term "humanity" as a reference to the experience we are living. There is an expression that is used frequently in metaphysical circles: "We are spiritual beings having a human experience." The experience of humanity is an illusion created to experience the separation from the Source. It is the realization of this fact that each Avatar of the past reached in order to step into the role of Avatar.

6

The illusion is created in thought, word and deed. It is the rending of separation that allows us to become the Christ, the Buddha, the Krishna, The Mohammed. Each of these enlightened Avatars laid down the illusion that is created through fear as an example for us to follow. In truth you must be "born again."

Children are fearless and love unconditionally. In coming to the state of love that we were as children, we are in fact seeing beyond the illusion. Watch an infant's eyes as they gaze around the room and notice when they notice things. Many times in your illusion nothing is there. The child sees far more than any of us.

"What you think, you become;" when Buddha spoke those words he followed them with "You create your world." The mere focus begins a creation. The conscious declaration of achieving your desire is asking of Source. And it is written "ask and you shall receive." Krishna in the Bhagavad Gita says, "When a person is devoted to something with complete faith, I unify his faith in that. Then, when his faith his completely unified, he gains the object of his devotion." Realize that you are creating in this moment. You are on the cutting edge of creation, on the bow of your ship, wheel in hand, on the sea of possibility.

"A dream is the bearer of a new possibility, the enlarged horizon, the great hope." ~Howard Thurman

This Moment

"Do not dwell in the past, do not dream of the future, concentrate the mind on the present moment." ~Buddha

Look around the room you're in, right now, go ahead do it. Realize that at this moment you are right where you are. When you look around the room it isn't yesterday nor is it tomorrow. It's not an

7

hour from now, nor an hour ago. This moment is the only one you have. The past is done. It is a collection of present moment memories, a track record of actions or inactions. The future is not set. In reality there is no future, there is only possibility. The future is a chalkboard on which we write goals. Each of those goals will not and cannot be achieved unless we take in the present moment. Right now in this present moment, decide what goes on the chalkboard - a new car, a new house, health, wealth, a loving partner. Make the decision and focus on the result of achieving that goal. Actively focus your thoughts on the final outcome of your desires. Realize that focusing on a specific partner entering your life is not productive as the person of choice may be focusing elsewhere. Focus instead on the perfect partner coming into your life and thus that partner will come. But realize that the action in this moment is the next present moment memory that you are creating. And the next will happen and the universe will surround you with like actions that will real-ize your dreams.

The Simplicity of Creation

"Progress is man's ability to complicate simplicity". ~Thor Heyerdahl

I recently received a message from an old friend. As I read her message I realized that probably ninety percent (maybe more) of the world doesn't understand that they are creating with God already. They don't tend to realize that when it was said "Ask and you shall receive" that you were already doing it. The difference is that Avatars like Jeshua, Buddha, Krishna, Mohammed and the like knew they could consciously create.

Unconscious creation is where the majority of the world is living their experience. I have said in earlier blogs that God's name is

8

"I AM" according to Moses. That being said again, your words are your tools of conscious creation. My friend's message said "I try and read [my blog] every day. I am desperately trying to renew my faith, I am having a hard time with it." From her statements I see that she doesn't read it every day, that renewal of faith is not happening and it is frustrating and that the attempt is very difficult.

When you declare "I am desperately trying," God will give you "desperately trying" because that is what was asked for in God's own name, I AM. Ask and YOU SHALL receive was what was promised, and so my dear friend is experiencing exactly what she asked for.

Conscious creation begins with listening. Listen to the words you use. A declarative statement is a creation that is on its way. If in the next moment you declare something contrary to your first declaration, the other is negated. But never fear, you're the one in charge of your thoughts. After a time of consciously shifting your words, your belief (faith) will follow. As results begin to be obvious so too will be your faith.

When the disciples asked Jeshua what diet they should follow, his response was, "I would worry more about what comes out of your mouth rather than what goes in." Spirituality is in the present moment. Religion is in the past. Stay in the present moment; realize that your words are creating with God right now. Change your words. Become conscious about what you are creating and realize that "How?" is not a question you have to ask, because God said, "Ask and you shall receive." He/She did not say "Ask and if you can figure out how, I'll give it to you." To ask is your job. The job of God/Universe/ Source/ Goddess is bringing it to your experience. If you need to know how, wait until it is in your experience then look back and marvel at the divine path to your experience.

If my friend declared, "I AM reading it every day. I am renewing my faith. I am having a fun time with it," what would she experience? What is she consciously creating with the above statements? The interesting thing is she was already directly creating with Source. The realization would come that all she has to do is shift to an optimistic creation and she would have the experience she desires.

Each of us is on the cutting edge of creation. We have the power to have any experience we desire. That was the promise. All we have to do is believe it and even that is our choice. I thank her for sending me the message; it gave me the opportunity to clarify.

God doesn't want followers. God wants creators. Go create joyfully and know we are changing the world for the better

"I focus on spiritual wealth now, and I'm busier, more enthusiastic, and more joyful than I have ever been." ~John Templeton

Optimistic Creation

"Every person is the creation of himself, the image of his own thinking and believing. As individuals think and believe, so they are." -- Claude M. Bristol

As the quote above says, we each are the architect of our lives. The way we create is through our faith, words and actions. Many times people have asked me how they can create the life of their dreams. All people really want the same things out of life: happiness, financial security, love, health, a nice home to live in. They look at their current situation and decide they are not where they would like to be.

I tell them about what I call "optimistic creation." Focusing on the negative aspects of your life and what you don't want, will only create that experience rushing into your life, because that is your focus. When creating a positive future, you have to be in an optimistic

10

state. Mother Theresa said "I was once asked why I don't participate in anti-war demonstrations. I said that I will never do that, but as soon as you have a pro-peace rally, I'll be there."

Consciously staying in the positive mind set can be a daunting challenge. People tell me they have a hard time doing it. I ask them if they meditate. Most of the time they tell me no. The majority of the people in the world don't believe they can meditate. They believe this for one very specific reason. When people try to meditate, they quiet their mind and then something happens. What happens is the events of the day begin to creep into their thoughts. The thoughts creep in and they realize it and shift back to being quiet. Then it happens again and again they shift back to the quiet mind. When it happens the third time they usually decide that they "can't meditate."

The people who become really good meditators are the people who continually release their thoughts and go back to being quiet until the quiet times last longer. It is the same with optimistic creation. When you find yourself creating any way other than positively, just recognize it and move back into consciously creating a positive outcome until the positive thoughts last longer and you real-ize the life you have chosen.

The interesting thing is that the reason we tend to create the way we do is we are unconsciously creating from our past experiences. When we shift into optimistic creation we are creating a trail of positivity behind us and so it only gets easier and easier. Two months down the road, you now have two months of positive past to begin unconsciously creating from. Jeshua said," Ye must be born again." I believe he was saying set down your past and be born into a new life. You can do so without unconsciously creating more of the same negative experiences.

The key to it all is not meeting a negative with a negative. When your negative thoughts invade your positive ones, recognize that it happened and shift back. Do not beat yourself up with self defeating thoughts. In fact, if you are the creator of your experience and you slip into creating anything but a positive outcome, think of it as just a silly occurrence. Recognize it as silly and laugh it off and switch back until your entire life is joyful and fun and prosperous. I look forward to witnessing the world you create.

"I focus on spiritual wealth now, and I'm busier, more enthusiastic, and more joyful than I have ever been." ~John Templeton

Change

"Do not be tense, just be ready, not thinking but not dreaming, not being set but being flexible. It is being 'wholly' and quietly alive, aware and alert, ready for whatever may come." -- Bruce Lee

As I have said many times, being present is extremely important. In healing sessions people are usually there because of the past. The past has many things, joyful moments, sad moments, and even bored moments. Each of these moments is just a step that has brought you to the present moment. We make decisions in the present moment. If we are not open to change, we will not progress. We will remain forever where we are if we do not try new things.

In the Bruce Lee quote above he says "not thinking but not dreaming." It is an interesting statement. I find it interesting because he is speaking of a moment of a sparring match, but there is much more to the statement. Dreams are fabulous, but unless action is taken in the present moment then none of your dreams can come to fruition. You have to be ready, not tense, but ready to move with your creation, to work with the Source. Bruce Lee also said "be like the nature of water."

In my life I have had many amazing things happen. Each has happened because I was open to the experience. I choose to be open, ready, alive, and take action in a micro-second. As big spiritual shifts began to happen in my life, I began to question whether I could or should be in a romantic relationship. I chose not to pursue that route. As I lived that way I discovered it was not for me. Up to as little as four weeks ago this was my mindset.

Four weeks ago I assessed my life and asked myself if the place I was in was fulfilling. I didn't think so. So I chose a new course. I asked God for a partner to walk with. As always God answered my prayer putting someone back in my life who has always held a special place in my heart. Come to find out that I held one in hers as well. Here was the moment of shift. I could have held steadfast to my celibate convictions or I could flow like the water, embrace the change and take the risk. Things are progressing very nicely with my friend and I could see it going somewhere. It would not be so if I had not embraced the possibility of change.

This is a funny quote and I am not even sure who originally said it: "The definition of insanity is doing the same thing and expecting a different result." If where you are is not working, do something different. Flow like the water as opportunities arise. Dreams are the goals, actions are the creations. Act as things are brought to your experience. Listen to the words of the song. Read the text with new eyes and act. Be ready for change and flow with the change as water flows around obstacles in the river.

You will find that once in motion life becomes easier. I thank you all daily for reading and hearing. I pray that these words can be an impetus for change if needed. I am honored that you have read them.

"The definition of Insanity is doing the same thing and expecting a different result." ~Albert Einstein

I Am Here . . .Now.

"You can clutch the past so tightly to your chest that it leaves your arms too full to embrace the present.: ~ Jan Glidewell

I am here. I am where I sit, in this chair writing. Each moment that passes I embrace with full expectation of positive outcome. The next moment is positive. We each create our experience in the present moment. When we remain focused on what was, or things we need to change, we are creating an experience with more of the same.

How do you feel? Do you feel nervous? Anxious? Sick? We each look down in the present moment and see the results of our past thoughts and actions. It is only in the present moment we can alter the experience that we are living. The mere act of observing our present condition is a baseline for change. When we start a motion in the present towards an objective, we begin the conscious creation of a life to come.

The real danger is slipping too far forward into the future mindset. Keeping our thoughts ever present brings about change, and a future of unbounded potential. When the focus begins a creation, the mind must be kept in the here and now; the constant observer of opportunity. Your creations are presented in opportunities. When you act upon them the creations come quickly. When you miss them another will present itself if you stay true to your initial creation.

The present moment is precious. It is the only true experience you have. Each moment is nothing but potential. The choice is yours as to what you do with it. Know that there are no limits, no boundaries, nothing to stop you from the greatest heights of your imagination. It is however only by staying present that the experience you seek can come to meet you.

"If you have one eye on yesterday, and one eye on tomorrow, you're going to be cockeyed today." ~ Author Unknown

Perchance to Dream

"To accomplish great things, we must dream as well as act."- Anatole France

Dreams, thought of as the children of an idle mind, can be just that. But more so they are possibility. I venture to say no one has ever achieved anything without some forethought or dream of a result. "The Secret" talks a great deal about interactive dreaming. They talk about imagining yourself in the car of your dreams, creating vision boards, and picturing it in your mind, all the while "feeling" the result.

Jeshua said "whatever you ask for in prayer, believe that you will receive it, and it will be yours." Active dreaming is a form of defining what you're asking for. Shop for the new home, define the house you want to live in, then dream of living in it. Imagine everyday things happening in that place. Imagine how comfortable you will be in the home. Decide what you are going to do with the interior design, the landscaping, decorations for the holidays. Dream yourself having gatherings of friends and weekend guests.

"Every great dream begins with the dreamer. Always remember, you have within you the strength, the patience, and the passion to reach for the stars to change the world." --Harriet Tubman

The more defined your dream and the more visceral the dream you create, the faster you will create that experience in your life. So dream not with an idle mind but an active creating mind that will send a ripple into the energy of Source, which in turn will surround you

15

with the experience. I am usually in the dreaming mode about one thing or another in my life. I am currently manifesting a wonderful new home with a loving relationship. As I asked for a relationship one was brought into my experience. Now I am focused on the home for that relationship to live in. I know full well that we will live that dream, since now we are both dreaming it.

What dream are you dreaming into your reality? Dreams are limitless as are the potential manifestations of your life. Dream big. Create big.

Living

"The supreme object of life is to live. Few people live. It is true life only to realize one's own perfection, to make one's every dream a reality"-- Oscar Wilde

Life - what is it? It depends on where you look. If you look backwards you'll soon discover that life is a string of moments, each building upon another leading to a current moment, the moment you live in. How have you lived each moment? Is your life the life of your past expectations? Is your life loving? Is it happy in your current moment? Take a moment and really assess where you are.

The string of moments behind you are what created your residual effect that you are currently living. If your life is headed in a great direction, wonderful. If in this moment your life is not where you would like to be, live your moment in a new way. How you live each moment creates the past and thus our beliefs of how the world is. We begin an unconscious creation of more of the same. This is a life of spinning your wheels. You work hard at it but still go nowhere.

Jeshua said, "Love one another." Each moment that we believe the world is a loving place brings a loving experience into life. Choose how you live each moment. Positivity breeds a new string of positive moments thus creating a new string of life experiences. Then after a period of time you begin unconsciously creating from a positive past which in turn creates more of the same. There is a theory that states it takes 21 days to create a new habit. If you could keep yourself in a positive loving state for a mere three weeks your new habit would be a positive loving life.

Today is day 21 - count down your days of positivity. If you start counting at 21 it feels as if you're already there, so by counting down it is only getting closer. By day 21 you'll find your life significantly altered if you will truly dedicate those 21 days to a loving positive life.

"Once you replace negative thoughts with positive ones, you'll start having positive results." --Willie Nelson

Born Again?

"There was a man of the Pharisees, named Nicodemus, a ruler of the Jews: The same came to Jesus by night, and said unto him, Rabbi, we know that thou art a teacher come from God: for no man can do these miracles that thou doest, except God be with him. Jesus answered and said unto him, Verily, verily, I say unto thee, except a man be born again, he cannot see the kingdom of God. Nicodemus saith unto him, How can a man be born when he is old? can he enter the second time into his mother's womb, and be born? Jesus answered, Verily, verily, I say unto thee, except a man be born of water and of the Spirit, he cannot enter into the kingdom of God. That which is born of the flesh is flesh; and that which is born of the Spirit is spirit. Marvel not that I said unto thee, Ye must be born again." -John 3:1-7

Born again? What does it mean? Man has pondered its meaning for centuries. He has marveled at the esoteric meanings of the words. He has condemned others by using these words. He has used them in order to feel superior to others. The interesting thing is the man who uttered these words said in no esoteric terms whatsoever, that we should not "marvel" that he said them.

Let's look at his meaning. When we are born into this world we are in the most physical state that we ever will be in our lives. We are truly of the earth and the earth has to provide for us, without us asking. As we grow older our intellect is developed, and eventually our search for what we believe begins. Eventually we must find answers to questions that have plagued mankind. Why are we here? Is there a God? As we begin our quest for the answers many turn to science to explain, more turn to religion.

Jeshua said, "Except a man be born again, he cannot see the kingdom of God." Interesting that religions have made this statement a major part of their ceremonial dogmas. In fact Jeshua never said that you should create ceremonies around being "born again." He said that you must be born again to see the Kingdom of God. It's interesting that he also said "The Kingdom of Heaven is within." If the kingdom is within, is he not referencing an inward journey to find the Source? We were born of the flesh in a very physical way and to discover our source we must find it within.

"God is Love," This says that the very essence of the Source/God/ Universe is Love and a joyful positive state. When we truly feel and express this state, it transcends pain and fear. Finding that love within as we have been told, is the very quest we are all here to conquer. Our physical birth left us feeling separate from the Source. In finding our way back, and being born into a more spiritual experience, we are truly finding the kingdom that is within.

"No one who has ever brought up a child can doubt for a moment that love is literally the life-giving fluid of human existence."--Smiley Blanton

If your life is hard, then you are expressing yourself as a person who believes life is hard. By dropping the physical experiences and the pain of separation, you have the ability to choose a new life of love,

18

easy, joyful love. That too is being born again, a new choice. This renaissance of self from a material world to a spiritual one will alter your perceptions and indeed your experience. Find the Spirit within and be born into a new life experience.

"Birth is the sudden opening of a window, through which you look out upon a stupendous prospect. For what has happened? A miracle. You have exchanged nothing for the possibility of everything."-- William MacNeile Dixon

The Way

"The way is not in the sky; the way is in your heart."-- Buddha

We each seek to find our way. It is in the search that we find it. For in the search we find that our worldly manifestations are just representations of our words, thoughts, and actions. We are, where we are, directly due to the way we have lived our lives. In accepting the responsibility of creation, we must accept also that circumstances not to our liking are also a result of our way of living.

When we make the transition to living a loving life we do nothing but enhance the world around us, as it is a representation of our way. Avatars of old told us they lived "The Way." Their lives were lives of love and compassion. Each told us that they themselves were examples of the way. Each expressed that the outer world is created within the individual, and so the Source of all is within us.

Living "the way" is to be loving and caring and truthful. Each Prophet, Messiah, and Avatar lived "the way." Each also lived the truth and the life that we are all capable of. Not only are we capable but each enlightened one asked us to live as they did. When Jeshua said "I am the way, the truth, and the life," his statement started with "the way." This implies that we should do as he did, because when we show someone the way we expect them to come along.

"I Am the Way, the Truth, and the Life"-- Jeshua

In coming along, our lives will be altered. We must accept the responsibility of the creations of our life, and move towards creating new and better present moments. Each step along The Way is deliberate and loving. That being said, loving things are deliberately created in our experience. This is what I call conscious creation, the deliberate act of creating a positive life for you and those around you.

"Whatever mishap may befall you, it is on account of something which you have done." --Prophet Mohammed

The Way does not have to be hard. In fact, The Way is really easy. Difficulties come when we focus on creating difficulties. When we focus and create love, joy, peace, then we find those aspects in our experience. Are you happy in your experience? If not, why are you doing that? If, as the Avatars said, we are creating our experience, then why would you be creating anything but happy? Focus your mind on the feeling of happiness, joy, love, security, and watch your experience change. Live the way you wish to experience life.

"Without the Way, there is no going; without the truth, there is no knowing; without the life, there is no living."--- Thomas Kempis

The Truth

"Believe nothing just because a so-called wise person said it. Believe nothing just because a belief is generally held. Believe nothing just because it is said in ancient books. Believe nothing just because it is said to be of divine origin. Believe nothing just because someone else believes it. Believe only what you yourself test and judge to be true." -- Buddha

When Sharon Prince first told me of my past life, I had an indescribable experience. It was so powerful to me, even more than the words she said. The experience was knowing the truth of it. Deep within myself I knew her words were true. This "knowing" was so profound for me that it began a real struggle with my belief system. Truth is truth - we each must judge what is our truth.

Raised Catholic, I grew up feeling guilty and afraid of hell and damnation. It didn't ring true to me and in fact, when I read the words "God is Love", I knew them to be true. Here is where my conflict began. If God is truly a loving deity, would he want me to be fearful or feel guilty? I do not believe so. My beliefs are of a simple oneness with God. I don't ask you if this is your truth. It is mine. If your beliefs are of a different sort then great, follow your path to the divine.

I truly believe that there is only one God/ Source/ universal consciousness, and we as thinking beings create our own illusions and structures around the divine. So if another illusion or structure is your truth then great. If, however, your structure or truth is such that it condemns mine or anyone else's, then I believe that that may be the place in your structure that needs examination.

"I am the Way the Truth and the Life"-- Jeshua

Many times I am condemned for my beliefs by others. I bless them along their journey to find God and wish them well. I will not condemn them for their personal beliefs. Why should I? They too are expressing their connection to Source. Find the truth in your faith. If it rings true to your soul follow it, share your beliefs with others. As soon as a judgment enters your faith, then my truth meter registers in the negative, and I choose to not believe that portion of your beliefs.

Truth - what is yours? Have you defined it, or are you still searching? Then searching is your truth. In seeking you will find. You find by listening to your own intuitions. Feel the truth within and it will indeed set you free of fear, doubt, and in fact, guilt.

My truth is Love, Unconditional Love, with all of its wonderful attributes: Respect, Honor, Happiness, Caring, Kindness, and more. In the end if God truly is love then I think that staying true to the Source can't be wrong.

"I believe that unarmed truth and unconditional love will have the final word in reality."-- Martin Luther King Jr.

The Life

"Dream as if you'll live forever, live as if you'll die today." -- James Dean

I spoke of the Way. I told you the Truth. Now I ask you to live your life in each and every moment. Find your truth and way. Express them through your every thought, word, and deed, creating the life of your dreams. Each truth that is put into action will enhance your life experience. When Avatars of old walked their truth, miracles were commonplace around them. The interesting thing is that each of these Avatars said that they were living the way, and that we are as capable of living the way as them. By holding fast to our truths, following them in all, and living it, we are truly spiritual and true to ourselves.

If your truth is that harmful or unkind things are acceptable, then those are the things that will befall you in your experience. If in faith you walk a kind, caring, joyful life, then your world will reflect those aspects. Your life experience will only be the one you desire, when in fact you live it.

"I Am the Way, The Truth and The Life"-- Jeshua

When Jeshua said those words he followed them with the much debated phrase "no man can come to the FATHER but by me." Or another interpretation: "no man can come to the FATHER but through me." My belief is Jeshua was an example, a template, an enlightened being who expressed our potential. The phrases above, I believe, state that he is the Way, not in a deification kind of way, but in an example kind of way. If he had been saying to deify him, why would he say such things as "Even the least among you can do all that I have done, and greater things" and "It is your faith that heals you."

Live your life as the Avatar. All the Avatars told you to. Create your life consciously and optimistically. Focus on a joyful life. A loving and happy existence. Show that to others and you shall experience it in your life. Carpe diem, seize the day and live each moment in love and appreciation. Namaste, My inner Avatar recognizes yours. May Allah be with you. Blessings upon you. I love you as Jeshua told us to.

"Take up one idea. Make that one idea your life-think of it, dream of it, live on that idea, Let the brain, muscles, nerves, every part of your body, be the full idea, and just leave every other idea alone. This is the way to success, that is the way great spiritual giants are produced."-- Swami Vivekananda

Tiramisu

"Look, there's no metaphysics on earth like chocolates." ~ Fernando Pessoa

I find myself looking for ways to explain some of my personal beliefs. I tend to use analogies as examples of comparable concepts. One such topic is that of the present moment creation. Many times I have said that if you ask for want, need, hope or try, what God will give you is wanting, needing, hoping, and trying. Some people have a hard time with this concept. The idea is based in focus. What you focus on you will bring into your reality, if you indeed stay focused.

One example of this: when I was married to my last wife I was adamant that I did not want to live in Pittsburgh and discussion about where we lived would always go back to the statement "anywhere but Pittsburgh." I gave focus to what I did not want and what happened? I could see the skyline of Pittsburgh from my front porch. My focus was on Pittsburgh and that is exactly what I got. Focusing on what you "want" is like asking God to not give you what you desire, because God lovingly gives you want.

"God gave the angels wings, and he gave humans chocolate." ~Author Unknown

Think of it this way: You're sitting in a restaurant. You've had a lovely meal. The server walks by and you say to them "I want dessert." Does the waitress get you the dessert of your desire? No. They cannot get your dessert until you say "I am going to have the tiramisu." One of these statements is a declaration of "want." The other is a declaration that will create the desired result. The server is God/Universe and they don't get your tiramisu with the first statement because you said you wanted dessert and as a good server, they serve what you ask for and you asked for "want." When you finally declared "the tiramisu" the server went into action to create that desired result. If, on the way to the kitchen you call out for the server and ask for ice cream instead, the tiramisu is forgotten and the ice cream will come to your table. The reason ice cream will come to your table is because in the present moment your focus switched and a new creation was begun.

"Ice cream is the original soul food." ~Lexie Saige

Complacency

"There has been a level of complacency that has helped the epidemic spread". ~ Deborah Levine

I talk a lot about the fact that you are the creator of your experience. I also talk about conscious positive creation and unconscious negative creation. The very nature of God/Universe is to be in motion. Say that we move forward in our lives, keeping positive and creating a positive outcome. God/Universe, a force in motion, would support keeping the creation in motion. If we, the creators, became complacent about our motion, God would begin unconscious creation mode and begin creating a new experience.

"It's not a very big step from contentment to complacency."~ Simone de Beauvoir

The very essence of conscious creation is focusing on goals and Holding faith that we would indeed create them into our experience. Complacency is a lack of focus, thereby creating a log jam. God in constant motion, flowing like water, finds the path of least resistance and continues creating. Complacency, being an indifferent state tends to create boredom. Boredom creates a desire for something else. Complacency being a less than joyful and actually a negative state tends to draw negative experiences into your life.

"If I stop, I'll die" ~Fannie Joseph

My ex-wife's grandmother was a wonderful lady. She would always say," If I stop, I'll die." Though this statement was spoken simply it has great truth behind it. We are here to experience life. When we stop our individual motion in a focused direction then we hinder our progress towards a positive outcome. Her statement basically said by staying in motion she was achieving her personal outcome: another day. Her life was a glorious one. Daily she would set tasks to achieve. The television was never on during the day and her house always had new projects going on. She lived into her mid-nineties and when she decided it was time to stop she did, in fact, pass on. She never became complacent, always sharing her stories of the day's project.

"Self-complacency is fatal to progress."~ Margaret Elizabeth Sangster

Forward motion with an eye on our joyful horizon creates a joyful life. Complacency creates stagnation and a negative outcome. Consciously bring that joyful horizon to you by staying ever in motion.

"I hate to see complacency prevail in our lives when it's so directly contrary to the teaching of Christ." ~Jimmy Carter

Never Too Late

"Remember, if you're headed in the wrong direction, God allows U-turns!" ~Allison Gappa Bottke

It's NEVER too late. If your life is on a track that feels as if it is headed to nowhere, turn around. We each tend to get into our life's travails, and then define ourselves by them, as opposed to defining ourselves as we wish. We can get to a point where we feel as if there is nothing we can do about our circumstance. It was we ourselves who created the circumstance. It is NEVER too late. Even the largest ships at sea can turn around. They turn the ship's wheel and slowly at first the boat seems to be continuing forward, but then its path alters and then alters some more. As the ship gets deeper into its turn the turning becomes easier. All of a sudden the view from the front begins to change. And they begin to see the wake they left behind. Do they steer the ship into the same wake? No. They do not because that water is still in motion, going in a different direction. It would be like riding a bike against the wind.

Many of us turn our ships into the wake. We return to the patterns of the past and wonder why we are not getting anywhere. We are reliving the life that put us on our previous course. The path back to happiness, to health, does not have to be a struggle against the current, for this too is choice. You can create anything.

"No matter what people tell you, Words and Ideas can change the world."~ Robin Williams

One of my favorite actors is Robin Williams.   I think he is brilliant and funny, but I am most impressed with his dramatic work in films like "Moscow on the Hudson," "The Fisher King," and "Good Will Hunting," for which he won his Oscar. I remember an interview I saw with him and one of the things he said has been something I have incorporated into my life. When asked if he would ever do a "Mork and Mindy" reunion show his response was "No, you never look back if you want to keep moving forward."

Nothing is insurmountable. Nothing is a game breaker unless we so choose it to be so. Who is steering your ship? Many will look at the analogy of the ship with a pessimistic point of view and say "but what if it's too close to land to turn?" To which my response is "Where did you choose to put your land?" You are the one creating your experience. It is NEVER too late. Create.

"He is able who thinks he is able" ~ Buddha

Metamorphosis

"They say that time changes things, but you actually have to change them yourself." – Andy Warhol

Change.   Change can be daunting. Without change we sit stagnant. Without it, eventually our situation would become boring. In propelling yourself forward to a new and exciting future change is inevitable. We, in fact, are in a constant state of flux in our experience, always in motion. Sometimes our motions are a repetitive act creating the same repetitive experience, thus giving the feeling of stagnation. Breaking this cycle is a simple as changing your mind.

Many times people come to me feeling as if they are "stuck". The statement "stuck" is an interesting one and usually my first response is "Why are you choosing that?" You see, to be "stuck" is to create stagnation. In choosing a "stuck" experience they are creating the experience of no motion because that is the focus of their thought. The simplest thing in our experience that we can control is our thoughts.

Metamorphosis is any complete change in appearance, character, circumstances, etc. When people feel as if they are not in motion, then they do not alter the experience, and so the appearance, circumstances, and indeed their character do not change. A true metamorphosis of the experience comes when they make a conscious choice. We are the creator of our experience. Choose change constantly, small change or large change doesn't matter, just continue to grow. A life in motion creates a joyful experience.

"It takes a lot of courage to release the familiar and seemingly secure, to embrace the new. But there is no real security in what is no longer meaningful. There is more security in the adventurous and exciting, for in movement there is life, and in change there is power." - Alan Cohen

We as humans tend to judge ourselves by our place in the world. The place we are in is a result of past choices. We become comfortable in our place because we are familiar with the place, and indeed understand how to deal with these circumstances. This creates what I call a velvet cage. It is comfortable inside but with no potential for flight. The bird in a cage will lose the ability to fly; its muscles become weak. Becoming comfortable in our personal velvet cages weakens our wings and limits our divine potential.

Open your cage and jump. Feel the stretch of your wings as they find new strength and soar to new heights. It is your flight plan, your journey. Ask for what you want from the Source, and embrace the change as it opens up before you. Do something that makes the muscles of your wings stronger....and fly.

"Change will not come if we wait for some other person or some other time. We are the ones we've been waiting for. We are the change that we seek." – *Barack Obama*

Breaking Belief

"What we are today comes from our thoughts of yesterday, and our present thoughts build our life of tomorrow: Our life is the creation of our mind." ~Buddha

Are you happy where you are in life? If so, congratulations - you have received what everyone strives for. True happiness is the simple connection to the divine. Is there anything you would like to be different? If not, I applaud your creation. Your current moment is the residual effect of all of your past thoughts and actions. Where you sit now is the creation of your beliefs.

Are you less than happy where you are in life? Are some areas of your experience frustrating or difficult? Maybe they are just not fun. These feelings are a direct result of your belief. It is your belief that creates your experience. If I were to walk through life believing the words of my father, in this moment I would be on the streets living as a "bum," having a frustratingly difficult time of life, because my belief would be supported by my creation.

Take this moment right now to assess all areas of your life. Assess each area one at a time: Relationships, finances, home environment. When you focus on an area what is your first feeling that comes over your body? That feeling is the signpost of your belief system. Does the thought of your relationships feel great? Does the mere mention of finances bring fear to the forefront? If you feel a negative (i.e.-anything other than a joyful happy feeling), then you have a belief that is keeping you in place and creating more of the same in the next moment. What is it in that negative experience that is the core of your belief?

Say I have my negative feeling surrounding finances. If I examine it closely I realize that the relationship I had with finances is a direct result of my parents' belief passed down. This is not to blame them, they came by their belief system honestly from their parents. The question is what would happen to my finances if I changed this belief?

"It is your faith that heals you."~ Jeshua Ben Joseph

The responsibility of your experience falls solely upon your shoulders. If you believe that life is a struggle, then a struggle is what you will receive. If you believe that life is easy and fun, then an easy and fun life you will receive. There is a statement I hear all the time that I think needs to be revisited: "Perception is reality." What we perceive we believe is the tenet of this statement. This statement and the belief in the truth of it, will perpetually keep us creating the same experience. What we are currently perceiving is the end product of our belief. Believing in that end product creates more end product and

30

thus a dead end in our creation. The truer statement would be "what we believe we perceive."

Find the belief that has you feeling stuck or stagnant in all areas of your life that have held you in place. Break that belief and set a new more positive belief. Hold that belief until you perceive the results in your experience. The life of your desire is a byproduct of faith.

"When we acknowledge that all of life is sacred and that each act is an act of choice and therefore sacred, then life is a sacred dance lived consciously each moment. When we live at this level, we participate in the creation of a better world." ~Scout Cloud Lee

The Tao of Popeye

"I aims to please." ~Popeye the Sailor

When looking back at heroes of my childhood, one stood out among many. Oh sure, Batman was cool and Superman was.....well... Super. But as far as a role model I have to fall back on the old stand-by, Popeye the Sailor. Here was a man with a lot going against him. He was short with misshapen arms and legs. He smoked too much. He was an obvious womanizer (though our tastes are quite different). He had one "squinky" eye. With all that going against the man he held true to a set of values.

When faced with adversity Popeye always did what was right. When a small infant was left upon his doorstep, he took the child in and raised it as his own. Later when a woman, one Olive Oyl, claimed to be the mother, he accepted what was best for the child and shared in the parenting responsibilities (though he did not allow her to rename Sweetpea "Baby Oyl"). When obvious nefarious characters came about with ill intent, Popeye stood between the child, its new mother, and the ruffian intending harm.

"I'm strong to the finich 'cause I eats me Spinach." ~Popeye

Though he had a definite disregard for his lungs, he did eat a proper diet, which included a lot of vegetables (mainly spinach). He was in obvious good physical shape as even his facial muscles could make a pipe spin like a boat propeller. This being said, he must have had physical conditioning far superior to many of their time. His dear friend Wimpy (God rest his soul) died of heart disease from too many years on the delayed payment hamburger diet. Though when Wimpy was in need, he always knew he could depend on his generous friend Popeye.

"I will gladly pay you Tuesday for a hamburger today." ~Wimpy

All this being said, Popeye's philosophy on life was a simple one, "I Am what I Am," he declared. This simple phrase can be taken in many ways. The first is as a statement of result: I Am in this moment the result of my past thoughts and actions. The Second is a statement of resolution: I Am in this moment all that I ever will be. The third is a creator statement: I Am what I choose to be. Hearing the grand tales of this legendary sailor, one must conclude that he stood firmly in the third option. As each seemingly insurmountable obstacle was placed before him, he stood firmly on his beliefs, putting himself in harm's way, and always being victorious. His life is a testament to what each of us is capable of. By choosing who we are in life and acting upon those convictions we create a chronicle of past "comic strips" that live as a testament of who we are.

"Oh Popeye, you're wonderful!!" ~Olive Oyl

Chapter 2. Fear

Fear is the opposite end of the scale from love. John Davis learned in his past life regression that fear was given to us by God as a tool to show us contrast. For isn't it true that we can't know what light is until we experience dark? We can't know what anything is unless we experience what it is not. The experience of fear illuminates the choice we can make in that moment: to choose to focus on the fearful thing and create more of that, or to focus on its opposite and therefore create the loving, joyful end of the spectrum. We can choose in this moment to react to a situation in fear, or ask in eager anticipation where this experience is leading us. Which is your choice? ~ HM

Words And Translations

Words fascinate me. They hold great power. I truly believe that the words people choose tell where they are in life. Words like "try" and "need" and "want" mean they haven't accepted the change they desire. The belief in words' meanings gives us our perception of their effect. Words like "Sin" and "Satan" conjure terrible images in the mind. These words hold us in places of guilt and failure confronted by an evil opponent. Sounds terrible, doesn't it?

If you look back at the original translations from the ancient texts an interesting thing arises. The ancient Hebrew word for "sin" literally translates into "guilt" while the ancient Aramaic word for "sin" translates to "failure". The ancient Greek word that has been translated into "Satan" only means "the opposition". The interesting thing to me is each of these words is a perception.

"Satan" stops being an evil villain and starts being someone of opposite views. "Sin" stops being a horrid action that we should be condemned for, but instead a perceived failure with guilt over failing. What was this horrible failure? The only thing we can judge ourselves so harshly over is not being loving. Now, we have to realize that these perceptions are concepts on a past timeline. It is in this moment we get to choose to do the loving thing. It is this moment we create our future. Walk away from guilt and failure. Make amends if need be (sometimes that is the loving thing to do). Don't let fear (the opposition of love) hold you in place.

"To some degree Satanism is purely a kind of disease of Christianity. You've got to really be Christian to believe in Satan." ~Alan Moore

Peter Pan Had It Right!

"Think one happy thought and you can fly" ~Peter Pan

Peter Pan had it right when he said, "All you have to do is think One happy thought and you can fly." There is an exercise we do in acting where you have a person imagine themselves to be a tree; when you attempt to lift them off the ground it is very difficult. When they imagine themselves in flight they are much easier to lift. If you watch a person who is in a depressed state of mind that person will feel heavier and are in fact harder to lift, whereas someone in a positive state of mind is easy to lift.

When we are in fear of any kind we are in a heavy place. When we are in love we can almost fly. Back in the sixties and seventies we would use terms like "that's heavy" or "that's a drag" when we heard negative news. Happiness is joy state, joy state is Love state, Love state is divinity/ Universe/ Source/ God. The interesting thing is we get to choose what we invest our time in. I choose positivity and love for all. See you in the clouds.

"You may shelve your Shakespearian plans for the present. I am going to play Peter Pan." ~Maude Adams

Judgment

"Judge not lest ye shall be Judged" ~Jeshua

I recently received an email from a woman who decided I was in danger from "The Evil One" and I was on a path "away from God, not toward Him." After reading the stories posted on www.JohnofPeniel.com, she decided that what I was doing was dangerous, saying that I was creating a whole new set of dogmas and religion. "No one can make up a religion like making your selection in the cafeteria line" she wrote. I responded that I respected her beliefs and honored her path, and thanked her for the concern.

She responded saying I was trying to glorify myself and that I was "insecure and ignorant." I am always saddened by the fear people feel, created by organized religions. I believe that the kingdom of God is within each of us and it is through our own doorway that we will reach the place of promise. Anyone who knows me knows that I never expect anyone to believe what I believe. I come to my beliefs through my own personal experiences and share them as a means for others to see they are not alone.

When one is raised in a fear based state, however, anything that is different from those beliefs is "dangerous." I honor the paths that each of us take to the Source but when I see people judge others for their personal beliefs it reminds me that there is a lot of fear in the world. Occasionally that fear will reach out and try to pull you in. She judged that I was dangerous, ignorant, and insecure because I did not believe as she did.

I explained that in her faith, Buddha, Krishna, Mohammed, Gandhi, and a myriad of others were currently burning in hell for their sins of not being Christian. She told me that she never found it to wrong to defend her faith. I asked who she was defending against as I had not contacted her. She had reached out to judge my faith in fear. I hope that our conversation has allowed her to look in love and not the opposing force, fear.

"People do not like to think. If one thinks, one must reach conclusions. Conclusions are not always pleasant." ~Helen Keller

As in all things I am grateful for the experience. I continue as I was, serving. I pray that she will choose to find the peace and contentment I have in my faith.

Friendships

"Assumptions are the termites of relationships." ~Henry Winkler

Over time friendships change. They start innocently enough, usually based on fun experiences. Over time you open yourself up more and more to your friends. You become relaxed, which is wonderful. It is a great experience, as it should be. When either you or your friend slips into fear, you begin to rely more and more on your friends until they become crutches for you. Interestingly, as they become a crutch for you, you become a crutch for them, enabling fear to live with you.

This life given to fear is a rapid spiral downward unless frequently checked. Each friend relies on the other to validate their worthiness. The need for validation is a product of fear. The spiral slips down further into fear and then when all else fails, the fear becomes directed at the other. Because the fear is now coming from one so close the damage is more. Boundaries are built and friendships alter. Each becomes less open to the other and a rebuilding has to begin, unless of course the friendships continue down the fear spiral into an ending of the friendship.

Doors do not have to stay closed to these ended friendships. No bridges have to be burned. Choose love over fear and accept that love is always correct. Take responsibility for your fearful acts. It is the only thing you can do. If the other decides to end the friendship, that does not mean you have to. Hold them in your heart in love. Always be their friend and in time that love will attract love in return. Sometimes they never return and stay mired in fear; love them all the more. For only love conquers fear. Walk into the light out of the fear and in love keep an eye for the friend lost in fear.

Always have your hand ready to pull them from the mire. The relationship will be different, probably stronger, but definitely different. God Bless all who fall into the spiral of fear and be a beacon for their return to love. I bless the friends of mine with whom this has happened and I ask forgiveness for my trespasses into fear and pray they will still have a hand out when I am in need.

"Condemn none: if you can stretch out a helping hand, do so. If you cannot, fold your hands, bless your brothers, and let them go their own way."
~Swami Vivekananda

Fear is The Devil

"There is nothing to fear but fear itself." ~Franklin Roosevelt

As I said in an earlier post, the word "Satanus" became translated to "Satan", but when linguists study it today they discover it means "an opposing force". I am a believer that God is love and fear is the opposite of love. Fear is the opposing force of love and love is God. Fear is the destroyer of lives, friendships, marriages, and relationships in general. Fear is the trespass for which we ask forgiveness. Fear is the trespass which we must forgive. To be in fear is painful. It hurts the heart, the mind, and the body. It damages lives. Pray that you not become tempted by your fear and lead into a dark place, a place from which you may not return. Remember you are in control of your fear. The "Devil" has no power unless the power is given to it.

"As a man thinks in his heart, so is he and so is the world wherein he dwells. Every man creates his own world according to that which he fears and that which he loves."~ Jeshua

Ask And You Shall Receive, No Matter How Much It Hurts.

"If life throws you a lemon - make lemonade". ~Joan Collins

One can never know how the Universe will grant your prayer. You ask for things and they are granted, but sometimes painful things are the impetus for change that puts you on the path towards that which you have asked for. An example: After years of struggling with my weight I asked God for healthy weight loss and a fit body. I immediately started feeling the symptoms of diabetes. It alarmed me. Being the spiritual person I am, and after seeing so many healings I knew that the power to heal was within. I began eating an 80% raw fruit and vegetable diet, which was something I had been planning on anyway for many reasons other than just my health. But change came quickly with the symptoms of illness, and the shift was made towards healthy weight loss and a fit body.

38

I also asked for the opportunity to get my spiritual work out there more, to be more of service. I immediately had a good friend abruptly end our friendship. I didn't want the friendship to end and still offer my hand in friendship to her. As soon as my friend decided to part ways, the Universe started bombarding me the right people to get my work out there more. A new friend with Internet marketing experience called me to tell me she is on "my team." Readers in California started recommending my services. Speaking gigs sprang up and more and more opportunities started to abound. It was as if I had to go through the painful process to get the result I had asked for.

I worked with a woman from Texas who asked for her child's father to step up and be a good father. Events took place that had her child taken from her so the opportunity would arise for the father to step up. The mother had shifted into a loving healthy life and the family around her erupted in fear, taking the child so the father could step up. The more fearful the mother becomes as a result of her lack of faith the more fearful events surround her.

Many people ask, but as soon as a painful event happens, they lose faith in the result. Remember that whatever you ask for you shall receive. So if you ask for something and painful things happen, they are just events that must play out to arrive at the desired destination. Be thankful for the pain, make the shift, and have faith you will arrive where you are supposed to be.

*"A man is insensible to the relish of prosperity 'til he has tasted adversity".
~Sa'Di*

Focus

"The key to success is to focus our conscious mind on things we desire not things we fear." ~Brian Tracy

Mother Theresa said "I was once asked why I don't participate in anti-war demonstrations. I said that I will never do that, but as soon as you have a pro-peace rally, I'll be there." Where is your focus?

I watched a YouTube video sent around by a friend. It focused on the violent riots around the world. It focused on fear of a "New World Order." It focused on all the negative aspects of fear and it was spread across the internet to spread fear. It will, I am sure, anger some, but more so I believe it will dishearten people and make them fearful, which is what was intended when it was made. If we focus on the negative we get more of the same.

How did Gandhi get the English to leave India? Through passive nonviolence in the face of extreme opposition. When you confront violence with violence it becomes an ignited flame fed by gasoline. It erupts and helps nothing. Focus is important. Bob Proctor says, "I don't care if it's get in or get out, if you are focused on debt you get debt."

Where is your focus? Are you focused on fear and violence? Is your focus optimistic or pessimistic? The ever optimist lives a joyful life. The ever pessimist lives a life in expectation of fearful events, and each receives reasons to keep believing as they do. I believe we can choose a new focus and the more of us that choose that can literally change the world.

"Change your thoughts and you change your world." ~Norman Vincent Peale

Don't Be So Serious

"Life literally abounds in comedy if you just look around you." ~Mel Brooks

Having spoken all over the country and experienced different types of religious thought, I have an interesting perspective on spirituality. In truly believing that God is Love, I believe that God is joyful. I find that most people who think of themselves as deeply religious are anything but joyful. They judge quickly and harshly out of fear. They get offended quickly, they are uptight and completely unhappy. I tend to look at the world through comedy goggles. I find things funny. I like to break the tension and make people laugh.

If God truly is love, would He/She want us to be judgmental, offended, or unhappy? As a loving deity would God not want us to be joyful always? The interesting thing is my approach to spirituality does tend to bring out the negative in these types of people. God is Love. God is Joy. God is Happiness. Judgment, being offended, or unhappiness is a quest for being right. If you are right, you are respected, if you are respected you are loved and so, being in the negative state is the fear of not having Love. God is Love.

It is written," Judge not lest ye shall be judged." If you look at that statement from a different perspective, negative attracts negative. If you judge, the mirror of the universe will mirror judgment upon you. By judging you are already judging yourself as judgmental. The place of judgment is raising yourself in status over someone else. It is the ego straining to get respect. Respect is love. It is the fear of not being one with God.

The message is simple: be Love. Love is joyful and fun. Love never judges or is offended. Love is always happy. When you feel any other way you have fallen into the ego trap of fear. Recognize it as fear let it go and return to Love. You are not separate from God. You don't need specific rituals or foods to know God. You just need to Love. As Jeshua said, "Love one another." When you are personally judged, you have a choice: you can be offended, unhappy and judge the person in return, perpetuating the fear, or you can respond lovingly and allow them to experience God. Most of what is said in judgment is based on religious belief. Remember that religion is the past and spirituality is the present.

"Don't worry, be happy." ~ Bobby McFerrin

Forgiveness

Forgiveness is choosing to love. It is the first skill of self-giving love. - Gandhi

Your past may be filled with memories that make you angry. Maybe the people who were to love you most were incapable of unconditional love. Maybe things were said or done to you that affect you even today. It is the effect that holds you in your experience. The fact that the memories carry such vehement weight means they are the anchors of unforgiveness. The keep you from sailing forward. When these events happened in your experience the "offender" was just another person like yourself trying to live and love just as you are. They made choices that affected you. Sometimes those choices were made subconsciously, patterns created by their offenders years before. It takes great strength to look at the offender as a vulnerable person, to see them as someone like yourself. Forgive them. Forgive yourself for thinking ill of them. They and you were only looking for love.

"The weak can never forgive. Forgiveness is the attribute of the strong." - Gandhi

Sometimes in looking for love, people will say or do the wrong things. These things can have lasting effect unless caught quickly. Recently in dealing with a new friend I came to the information that they had lied in order to make themselves appear more important. I

42

came to realize that they had told the untruth to be respected and thus loved. I forgive them for the lies. I walk away with knowledge. Knowledge that the truth shifts easily in them and that I must not take their words as truth. I forgive myself for thinking ill of them and move forward wisely. I love this new friend as another person finding their way, for I am sailing onward to my personal enlightenment and I leave the anchors of resentment behind.

"When you hold resentment toward another, you are bound to that person or condition by an emotional link that is stronger than steel. "Forgiveness is the only way to dissolve that link and get free."-- Catherine Ponder

Worry

"Which of you by being anxious can add a cubit to his height?" ~ Jeshua

In our lives situations, circumstances or events occur that tend to make us worry or become anxious. This is the moment of recognizing the fear. When times like that happen, be grateful, for that moment is the moment of great change and possibility in your life. You can create wondrous and joyful things in these moments by just keeping your faith in a joyful life, and realizing that the moment of anxiety is just a necessary moment of shift.

By focusing on the worry or anxiety you are in fact creating more things to worry about. It is a futile response that propagates the anxiety. Does the worry help anything? Does the worry feel good? Are you happy or joyful when anxious? Why do it? It is just fear, and it was given to you as a tool. Is the carpenter ruled by his hammer? "In Anxiety" is "In Fear" it is you giving control to fear. Realize that you are actively giving the control away and you can actively take it back. You are the only one who can.

"Drag your thoughts away from your troubles... by the ears, by the heels, or any other way you can manage it." ~ *Mark Twain*

By actively keeping your thoughts in a positive frame, you are negating the fears. Eventually the fearful thoughts become less pervasive in our minds. Then as times of anxiety do occur, we approach them with a new perspective, one of objectivity. Think of your feelings as data. You feel one way or another because of your beliefs, your faith. By approaching the feelings scientifically we can find our truest beliefs.

In truth, it is our faith that creates our world. It is our unconscious faith that takes us into anxiety. I say this because you didn't choose to be worried. Did you choose to feel anxious? It was an unconscious response created within your belief. By detaching from the fear emotionally and recognizing it as data, you now have the tool to set your fear down.

In the sixties they used to say "What a drag," "That's heavy" or "That's a downer." These heavy feelings are the fears affecting your very being. By actively releasing fear we become en-lightened. Don't worry about worry.

"Worry bankrupts the spirit." ~ *Berri Clove*

Trust

"Faith is not belief without proof, but trust without reservation." ~ *anon.*

Trust can be the force that stops a person from living a joyful life. In my life I have been married twice; each ended finding out that my spouse was unfaithful. Trust has been a big issue in my life. It is an interesting word, trust. Like most words it can have both positive and negative connotations. If someone is very focused on trust, then are

44

they truly being trusting? When someone is hurt by another in such a painful way as infidelity, it can paralyze them with the fear of being hurt again.

At times like this, the actuality is that they are choosing fear. "Trust" becomes the poster child of fear. "How can I ever trust someone again?" or "Can I trust you?" become common thoughts, and phrases for the person in fear. We decide we can't trust, and so we make decisions that keep us safe from our fears. In my personal case, I decided to become celibate. It was safe. I didn't have to trust again.

To trust another is to completely render yourself vulnerable. How can you truly live your life without releasing the fear, and trusting? Relationships suffer because of the lack of trust, but trust is a choice. It is the choice of the person who is giving the trust. To release your fear and trust is to allow the good things to come rushing into your life.

"Every time we choose safety, we reinforce fear" ~Cheri Huber

I recently entered into a new and wonderful relationship. I felt pangs of love for her, and immediately began fearing that love being false, or worse yet, that I was unworthy of it. I decided first of all that I needed to trust love. If I trusted love, and nurtured love, then love would be what I was creating in my life. I informed my girlfriend Kelly that I was dealing with trust issues, and that they were my issues, and they had nothing to do with her. I know full well that she was not only trustworthy, but the one that I loved and trusted. It was my issue because they were my feelings and as such I needed to deal with them.

As with any change in life it takes some time to create the muscle memory to release the fear. I had to force myself to let go of the fears from the past, and trust this amazing person who has brought a level of joy back into my life that I had dismissed as folly. I allowed myself to be vulnerable, all the while informing her of what I was going through. This process of working through issues with your partner helps build trust as they are the one you are sharing intimate secrets of your vulnerability with. They become the "trusted" confidant, and your trust builds alongside the growth of your relationship.

Trust is like a relaxing exhale when you first give it fully. The lack of trust is just a symptom of fear. I love my partner Kelly, and my faith in her is proven every day as she helps me through my issues. I breathe easier every day as we create a beautiful future built on a foundation of love, mortared with trust.

"We're never so vulnerable than when we trust someone - but paradoxically, if we cannot trust, neither can we find love or joy." ~ Walter Anderson

Suicide

"Death is no more than passing from one room into another. But there's a difference for me, you know. Because in that other room I shall be able to see." ~Helen Keller

Last night someone very dear to me lost a close friend to suicide. I don't want to go into names because they like their privacy and don't like to be fawned over. I am also keeping the victim's name to myself because I want to respect who he was in life, not in the tragic end.

When people become so trapped in fear they can't see the way out, they fall into a mindset that is erratic. They can not see that love is all around them, and in performing the terrible feat of suicide they don't realize how much they hurt all those people. Sometimes, they even feel that they must kill themselves to stop hurting others. The reality of it is, he was afraid. No one caused the fear; he himself allowed the fear to consume him. I feel great sorrow for the desperation that lead to his death.

"As anyone who has been close to someone that has committed suicide knows, there is no other pain like that felt after the incident" ~Peter Greene

Those who knew and cared for him are now playing the "what if" game. "What if I did this," or "I only wish I saw it coming," become common phrases for the ones trying to cope with the act. Suicide is selfish. It is a direct response to fear. It is the result of completely turning inward and having no regard for those around them. When I hear the stories of this man, they are not of a selfish man. The stories are of a fun-loving, scattered individual who was loved by his family and friends.

"If you throw someone a life preserver, and they turn around and swim away from it; what can you do but let them drown themselves." ~anon.

I lost a cousin years ago to suicide. I can remember vividly the last time I saw him before death. He came into the room I was in and said, "I just wanted to say goodbye." He then turned to leave, did a double-take, almost came back, but shook his head in decision and left. His name was Carlos and he suffered the pain of depression. His life was very hard, but when you thought of him, he was fun-loving, sometimes scattered, and loved by his family and friends. Months later, I was staying at my parents' home in the darkest bedroom in the house. In that room I saw a bodiless aura form, and intuitively, I knew it was Carlos. My mind flooded with the knowledge that I needed to get a message to his mother. The message was, "I am in a better place now." The opportunity presented itself a few weeks later. I began to prepare her for the message by finding out her beliefs and then came my chance. "I saw Carlos," I told her. She paused and then asked, "Is he in a better place?"

He is in a better place, as is my friend's friend. Here, they were both trapped in their fears, struggling with them daily. There they are embraced in unconditional love without fear. They can rest from their pains and feel the ecstacy of the pure God/Universe. The best way to honor them both is to not dwell upon the fear they represented in the end, but focus on the fun, loving, sometimes scattered friend they were in life. Another way to honor them is to live your life as fun, loving, and joyful, because that is how they liked you best.

To my most dear friends in pain today: I love you and always will. Find joy in the times you shared. Don't give power to the fear that took him by reliving what he did.

"The fear of death follows from the fear of life. A man who lives fully is prepared to die at any time." ~Mark Twain

Inheritance

"The key to change... is to let go of fear."~ Rosanne Cash

Each of us walks through our life trailing our fears behind us. Many of our fears were established by the events of our lives; many were established by events in our parents' lives. For example, if our parents had a trauma that made them afraid of fire, they might pass that fear onto us as children. Our beliefs would be established by their fears, and thus we would carry that fear of fire with us throughout our lives.

We each have these fears within us, but it is through the conscious release of these fears that we move forward. Respect for fire is a good thing, but general fear of fire would and could make a great number of potentially wonderful events in our lives uncomfortable. Bonfires would be frightening. Gas stoves would tend to raise a pit in the stomach, and so on.

As parents we need to take great care not to pass this inheritance of fear to our children. If one pair of pajamas is less flammable than another, does the child need to know that? No. That child does not need to think about the fact that they might catch on fire, thus creating that possibility all the more. Instead allow the child to sleep in their "nighttime clothing" and let the fearful thought of fire be healed within you, thus ending the cycle.

The Law of Attraction is a hot topic now. Think about this: if, in fact, it is a "law", then the focus on fear would be bringing that reality into being. Have you ever seen someone afraid of heights near a high edge? They become much more clumsy and awkward as they approach therefore creating a greater possibility of falling. The fears of our parents are our fears. Now that we have allowed them to be our fears, we continue the cycle, and hand that fear down the line. The cycle will remain unbroken until someone takes action.

"What we seek we shall find; what we flee from flees from us." ~ Ralph Waldo Emerson

Our feelings tell us directly when we are in fear. When we are fearful we feel negative and unpleasant. When we are not in fear we feel relaxed, and joyful or content. By recognizing the feelings of our body, we can recognize these times of fear, and consciously relax our bodies, breathe deeply and let go. The fear dissipates. Through breath control and relaxation, during these times of fear and stress, we create a new muscle memory and new ways of thinking, ending the cycle.

The life of your dreams is easily achieved once the fear is released. Like the anchors of ships, when they are let go, they allow the ship to sail forward. Fears can be debilitating to a life's progress; we already have the tools within us to move beyond the fear.

"You block your dream when you allow your fear to grow bigger than your faith." ~ Mary Manin Morressey

Religious Militant Fundamentalism

"Fundamentalism as it is called is not confined to the Muslim world. It is something that we have seen in different parts of the world. Let us hope that a dialogue between the followers of the three great monotheistic religions could help in putting an end to this." ~King Hussein I

I was recently sent a link by someone who proclaims to have "light worker" status. Unfortunately, the link that was sent was an absolute attempt to spread the fear of militant fundamentalists. I say this because the message sent out was a message that one should fear the Muslims. I have met many Muslims in my travels abroad and found each of them to be the same as you or I.

When traveling through Egypt, I went to Mt. Sinai. While there I befriended the manager of the hotel where I was staying. I showed him respect and friendship, and he returned it in kind. The following day after climbing Mt Sinai, I ran into another American. "Are you having any problems here?" he asked. "Not at all," I responded. "You're lucky, everywhere I go they all want to fight me," he continued. As the conversation went on I began to understand; by the end, I wanted to fight him. He was putting out a fearful lack of respect for the people of Egypt, and they were returning it in kind. In fact, the night before as I began climbing Mt. Sinai, the Manager I told you about ran up the path a quarter mile from the hotel to give my traveling companion a coat because he said it would be freezing at the top.

"He who knows not kindness has no faith" ~the Prophet Mohammed

The individuals who look at others of different faiths in fear are, in fact, amplifying the fear. That can only lead to an explosive result. There are Muslim fundamentalists just as there are Christian fundamentalists. Our last President told the Saudi prince that, "God told him to invade Iraq." The wielding of religion and God for aggressive actions is a medieval premise that should not be tolerated in a shifting world.

The question is which way do we want to shift our world? Do we want a world based in fearful aggressive actions or of peaceful loving actions. As long as religious fundamentalists create out of fear and we do not take notice, then our world has no choice but to head into a dark valley of fear. Let us peacefully put out our hands in love, and actively shift the world in a positive direction, fulfilling the actual intent in being a light worker.

"Love one another." ~ Jeshua Ben Joseph

Many will say they do not know how to combat militants with love. I say this, read everything you can about Mahatma Gandhi. Whenever things in his country went violent, he did a nonviolent counter action. What did he achieve - a free India. The spreading of fear by "lightworkers" should show fully where their truth is. Are they living a life of light while they spread fear? It is impossible to be a light worker if in fact the fruit you bear is darkness. Gandhi said, "Be the change you want to see in the world." If you want a world without fear then don't fear. If you want a world of fear and violence then spread the fear and violence. I find it sad that many on the "spiritual path" are using their religion or spirituality as a means of power or control.

"Be the change you want to see in the world."~ Mahatma Gandhi

Eventually the seeds of love and peace that we spread will burst forth into the representation of the tree of life. The seeds of fear can spread like a parasite, but we can prune them away easily and keep the light on our tree. Christians and Muslims can be friends. I have seen it with my own eyes. It is all the same Source that we all come from. When we take the Love out of God, then we turn our backs on him/her fully because "God is Love."

"Love is all you need"~ John Lennon

Chapter 3. Faith

Faith is a term we usually hear in the context of religious doctrine – a belief system. The dictionary also defines faith as complete confidence or trust in a person or thing. It is important to recognize that true faith is not "hope," is not "maybe," is not "potential." True faith is knowing, believing, an absolute trust. Those of us who have based our feelings in our present lives on events of the past often base our current trust on those past experiences, for good or ill. Those of us who base our lives on this moment of creation, this moment of knowing, can choose the fear or the love response. When we let go of past experience and base our lives on what we choose to create in this moment, we reinforce our faith – faith in ourselves and faith in the Universe to provide what we ask for. We can choose in this moment to react to a situation in fear, or ask in eager anticipation where this experience is leading us. Which is your choice? ~ HM

A Broken Tooth Moment

"Of the blessings set before you make your choice, and be content." ~Samuel Johnson

To say I needed some dental work done would be an understatement. The dentist had told me that the cost to repair my mouth would be between $9,000 and $12,000. As a professional speaker I wanted to get it done so as to not have a bad first impression with clients. As always I turned to my faith in God/Universe and prayed my usual prayer formula: Thank you God for the perfect teeth I AM receiving. The next day I was eating a sandwich from a local deli. When I bit into the sandwich my left front tooth broke off in the sandwich. This tooth was a crown that had been in my mouth for over two decades.

Looking at my broken tooth I had a choice. Would I say "Well THAT didn't work!" or would I choose to keep my faith and say, "I wonder where this is leading me?" I chose the latter because I asked and my faith is that when I ask, I receive. An hour later the phone rang. It was my friend Gracie. "What's going on?" Gracie asked. "Well, my tooth broke off," I responded (which I wouldn't have said if it hadn't). "Really? Let me tell you about my dentist," she answered. She went on to explain that her sister owned a house a short distance from the Mexican border in Texas and that just across the border the dental work is 25% the cost in the U.S. "That's great but I still would have airfare and lodging," I said. Gracie went on to explain that I could stay at her sister's, who is also a good friend of mine, so lodging wasn't an issue. I still was dubious about a positive result.

I arranged to see a different local dentist to see if I could get the newly broken tooth fixed. After a short dental visit informing me that the one tooth alone was going to cost $3000 to fix, I left the office, still holding my faith. "Thank you God for the perfect teeth I AM receiving," I repeated. As I drove home a word kept coming into my mind: "rescue." It got louder and kept coming until I realized that the word was RESCU (an organization for Renaissance Festival participants who need financial help for medical bills and such). I called RESCU. "Hello, this is Carol," a voice came back to me that I immediately recognized. Carol was a long time friend and currently the president of RESCU. I shared with her my dilemma and she told me she would discuss it with the board. She took it to the six member board of RESCU, most of which I knew and were friends. They awarded me $3000 which I took to Texas with me and had the majority of all the work done at 25% the cost it would have been in the States. I still have a few things to do but I am well on the way to the perfect teeth I have faith I am receiving.

54

Remember that when things do not seem to be going the way you asked them to go, hold on to your faith. Your "broken tooth moment" is just what has to happen for you to receive the answer to your prayer.

"To me, success is choice and opportunity." ~Harrison Ford

Daddy, I Know Everything.

"Imagination is more important than knowledge." ~Albert Einstein

Tonight at dinner my five year old professed to me, "Daddy I know everything." "Do you?" I responded. He smiled and told me he did. "What is everything?" I asked. "I know that apples and cherries are red," he confidently snapped back. He knew full well that his response answered my question. He was sure the conversation wouldn't continue down that vein. "Is that everything?" I continued, just to see where it would go. "It's enough" was his response.

Our experiences are draped with knowledge. Each one of us has had multiple experiences as have our families and friends, friends of friends, and neighbors and so on and so on. I have a faith that tells me we are all connected. We are more than what our mirrors reflect back to us. As one, the knowledge must be a communal property, a shared file. Psychics for years have delved into the universal consciousness to pull information during readings. Here was my five year old telling me he knows everything. I think he is right, and as he delves deeper into his interests, the knowledge will be there for the plucking. Like an apple or cherry from a tree. The knowledge is there for the taking. Pluck what is "enough," and be grateful for the resource of universal knowledge. At five years old, that apples and cherries are red is enough. He made me smile.

"Break open a cherry tree and there are no flowers, but the spring breeze brings forth myriad blossoms." ~Ikkyu Sojun

Where U At?

No matter where you are in life, you arrived there through your past thoughts and actions. Actions are a response to our beliefs. We react according to our beliefs. If we believe our life is lacking, then our actions or inactions create a life of lack. If we believe our life to be fun and adventurous then our actions will create that experience.

Your life changes with your very thoughts. Discover fully what your beliefs are. Listen to your words. You cannot manifest wealth if you are constantly searching for the way to make money. Believe you are receiving it and when your belief shifts to absolute faith, your actions will be congruent with the result you are creating. After your belief/faith has a track record it will create it fully. When you focus on "how" then you are creating lack; your belief is you aren't receiving it because you don't know how. Release "how" and have faith that it is coming. You are unlimited, as is the Universe. Nothing is too big or too small. In my life I wanted to travel. I had complete faith I would. I never asked how. I just had faith I would. I have been to twenty-seven countries, most of which I did not pay for. I have been inside the great Pyramid of Egypt and climbed Macchu Picchu and Mt. Sinai. I did not know how I would get there but I went because my faith was that I would get there. Start manifesting what you want. Bypass the "how" moment and step into the receiving moment.

They Are Your Beliefs.

"I am what time, circumstance, history, have made of me, certainly, but I am also, much more than that. So are we all". ~James A. Baldwin

Our lives are created by our beliefs. What we believe becomes our reality. In our lives we choose what we believe and yet many of those beliefs come from people in whom we place power. Doctors find cancer, they tell the patient they have cancer and how they are going to fight the cancer. They give odds and sometimes even predictions of a death date. As they are more learned than we, we tend to believe their predictions. Death comes.

I am reminded of a magnificent person named Maria. She came to me with a death prediction of six weeks. Together we shifted her beliefs and today almost a decade later she is still with us, cancer free, and happy. We are the master of our experience. Our fears create dis-ease. Our beliefs in the disease empower the disease. No matter who says what, you are still the one who chooses to believe. They will tell you many things. The things they will tell you are all based on your past thoughts and actions, on your beliefs. I say this because they are looking at the results of your unconscious creation. The conscious shifting of your beliefs will shift your experience. Health and well being can be yours if you so choose.

A dear friend and extended family member today received news of lung cancer. The doctors removed a third of one of his lungs today. Tomorrow we begin the shifting. I spoke to him before the biopsy and we began the shift of belief. Now the real work begins, the shifting of belief after a doctor's prognosis. If he chooses so, he will be healthy and vibrant again.

Remember they are YOUR beliefs. You do not have to accept anyone else's. Believe in a joyous life of health and prosperity and SO

BE IT. Blessings to you all for the choices you make. Choose Love for yourself, others, and the world.

"Man is made by his belief. As he believes, so he is."~Johann Wolfgang von Goethe

Knowing

"It is not the mountain we conquer but ourselves." –Edmond Hillary

"Ask and you shall receive." Your life is unlimited potential. In fact, the only limits on your experience are the limits you set. Faith in yourself is key to unlocking the vault of your potential. If you believe you will achieve something, you will.

On healing days, I sit in the room talking to the person in need. They tell me the issues that brought them to a "healer." I listen to the words as they flow forth. Their words tell me their faith. Whatever they believe they are creating in their experience, they each ask for health. I tell them that they are the ones with the power. All they have to do is know they can. "Whatever you wish, ask and it is granted." If you ask it is granted. I tell them that declaring the truth that they are in fact healed will heal them. But the simple confidence that they can is the truest faith they can have. Earlier in the day each one knew with complete faith that they were coming to see me. They each got up, got dressed, probably said to someone, "I am going to see a healer," and they walked out the door, got in the car, and drove. Eventually they ended up sitting in a chair across from me. They manifested sitting there, and did so in God's name, "I AM going to see a healer." If we each take this kind of simple faith in our manifestations then they come quickly.

"You must do the thing you think you cannot do"—Eleanor Roosevelt
58

Knowing that you can is a gift you can give yourself. If you are limited only by the limits you set, then set them higher. When I was younger, I had an old beat up Chevy van. The body of the van was rusted out, but the motor and transmission were good. My father had a dead van in the driveway that had a good body, but bad motor and transmission. I bought it. Up until this point I had only changed oil and spark plugs. I knew nothing of mechanics. I called my family's most valuable asset, my brother-in-law Buddy. Buddy is a man who can do anything mainly because he has a belief that he can.

Buddy confidently told me "get started and call if you need help." I pulled the vans side by side and proceeded to take them apart. Marking and listing each part as it came off, I continued. My father's van was a three speed on the column, mine an automatic transmission. I discovered I also needed to swap the steering column. I continued until finally the day came when I thought I had completed the job. I had never called Buddy. I got in the van and tried to start it . . . nothing. I looked for any problems, nothing. I called Buddy. He arrived and began looking at what I had done. "That's right, that's right, that's right," He got behind the wheel, turned the key, nothing. I looked under the hood and all at once the van fired to life. "What was it?" I asked. Buddy responded, "Well John, you have the only automatic van that you have to push the clutch pedal in to start." I had forgotten to take out the clutch pedal and the switch that will not allow you to start it in gear was still there.

I knew I could as I went through the process. I didn't doubt what I was doing. I just did it in faith. I only made one mistake which was remedied in the next hour. A week later I drove that van to Georgia from Delaware. My sister and her husband drove that van for years after.

Have faith. It is the same faith to say "I am going to the store" and doing it, as it is to swap an engine, transmission and steering column with no prior experience. All you have to do is know you can and do it. And you will achieve greatness in your life.

"Nothing splendid has ever been achieved except by those who dared believe that something inside of them was superior to circumstances."—Bruce Barton

Patience

"Patience is the companion of wisdom" ~Saint Augustine

What is your faith? Do you believe the world a good place or a bad one? A true test of your faith is the level of patience you have. Many people you deal with in the world are full of fear and see the world in that very way. If they spew their fear in your direction what is your response? The person of true faith knows that the essence of God/Universe is Love. They also know that they can walk through the valley of fears and patiently observe the fear around them. It is their faith that allows the patience. Why would one become impatient if everything is truly Love?

The person who carries that much faith will possess the ability to create any experience they wish. You see by faithfully holding love there is no alternative but patience. I say this because allowing yourself to focus on the negative aspects of life will only bring them rushing towards you. The one who stays truly focused on a loving abundant world can receive their heart's desires.

"He that can have patience, can have what he will." ~Benjamin Franklin

Your world is created by your belief. If you believe that the world is just stimuli that you respond to, then you give up control to

60

the stimuli. If, however, you patiently remain the observer and realize the negative stimuli is just fear, then your "patience pays."

I have been a director at renaissance festivals around the country for many years and one trait a director of shows like this must possess is patience. I remember a moment a performer came up to me, stood nose to nose with me and called me every name in the book. When I say every name, I mean every name. His finger was two inches from my nose as he accused me of doing things with my mother that I didn't even want to imagine my father doing. I stood there and let him say every word. I never let my temper flair in response to his fear based tirade. After he was finished I gently and lovingly talked to him and heard his grievances. I told him I would look into the matter.

About fifteen minutes later he walked up to me and very gently apologized for the way he spoke to me. You see he was in a fear based place and by my recognizing it, by staying ever present, I was able to express the patience and the love to allow him to have his fear moment. By not feeding the fear it was able to dissipate and was released.

"The keys to patience are acceptance and faith. Accept things as they are, and look realistically at the world around you. Have faith in yourself and in the direction you have chosen." ~Ralph Marston

Have faith that your world is a fun, loving, and enjoyable world and patience will become your way of life. Because your experience is created by your choice. Choose Love over fear with full faith and when fear expresses itself, you will love it out of your experience . . . patiently.

Daddy, I Know Why You Keep Missing.

"Faith is spiritualized imagination." ~Henry Ward Beecher

I am a proud father of the greatest six year old kid in the world. He always amazes me with his wisdom. Many times the information that comes from him is funny. Recently for example, I was informed that the word, "poo" was a secret word for the word "poop." Other times his words take my breath away in a much more enlightened way.

Last night we were playing with his new nerf crossbow. We came up with a great new game. One of us sits on the couch in the living room and tries to hit the side of the kitchen trash can with a nerf arrow. The other one stands half way to the kitchen door with two nerf swords flailing up and down to try and stop the arrows. For some reason when it was my turn I kept accidentally (wink) missing the target. I was really bad shot. Kynan, however never missed hitting it every time.

One time, while I was up trying to stop the arrows, Kynan laughed and said, "Daddy, I know why you keep missing." "Why?," I asked. "Because you don't believe," he said. I smiled, "What do you mean?" "You have to believe you're gonna hit it." he continued. He stopped, aimed his arrow (me all the while flailing the swords up and down) and fired. The arrow shot straight through the nerf swords and struck the side of the trash can. Kynan later told me that he was a "good believer," and I wasn't as good at believing as he was.

Faith is just belief. Belief is just choice. Kynan's simple message was beautiful. Believe you will reach your target and you will. If you do not believe, you won't. Decide to believe you will receive what you ask for. Jeshua said, "Whatever you ask in prayer, you will receive, if you have faith." The faith is the important thing. Ask, believe and receive. That is the straight poo (wink).

"Belief creates the actual fact." ~*William James*

✳

Faith

"Faith is to believe what you do not see; the reward of this faith is to see what you believe." ~ Saint Augustine

We put faith in many things. When we eat our favorite food we have full faith that it will taste wonderful as it crosses our taste buds, and indeed it does taste great. The question is, would it have tasted great if we believed it was something other? If, as Buddha says, our thoughts create our world, then it must be so to the tiniest degree. We decide whether we like a thing or not and so it is until we change our belief.

If it is so with the tiniest of things in our reality then it must be so with the largest as well. To put full faith in a grand dream is to bring it into creation. Big or small does not matter, because matter is made up of tiny particles. The particles in the big things are the same exact particles that make up the small things as well. Our dreams seem daunting in size and scope, but in reality if our faith can grasp it then it can be brought into our experience.

Believe that your dream is right here in the present moment just as your favorite food tastes great. That is the key to manifestation. Leave behind the illusion of large or small. It is all small. The creation of a big dream is as simple as breathing or sleeping. Focus in full faith then hold the dream until it is in your reality.

"To me faith means not worrying." ~John Dewey

That we find bringing our dreams into reality daunting is evidence of our fear of not achieving them. We worry about "how" or "when" or worse yet "if only." Do you worry about how your favorite food will taste? You have full faith and so it is so. Release your worry, your concerns, your fears and real-ize your dreams. You'll then find the more you release the fears and stay in the mindset of creator that it will become easier. Your creations will be positive and so you unconscious mind will begin creating your positive experience around you. Just as effortlessly as grass grows, your experience will expand in miraculous ways.

Go create.

"As your faith is strengthened you will find that there is no longer the need to have a sense of control, that things will flow as they will, and that you will flow with them, to your great delight and benefit." ~Emmanuel Teney

Focus Then Release

"Creation is only the projection into form of that which already exists."
~Bhagavad Gita

All the books on manifestation speak of focus being of utmost importance. It is a major part of it to be sure. After focus comes another all important step as well - release. I jokingly say that many of the modern religions teach their followers to pray as if they are waiting. They continually thank for the result of their prayer. The continual focus on the gratitude does not convey the fact that they have the result. In fact, it conveys the opposite.

"Whatever you ask in prayer, you will receive, if you have faith."~ Jeshua

When Jeshua spoke those words, I believe he meant them. To be in continual gratitude holds us in the place of lack. The example I use is this: when you ask for a glass of water and someone gives it to you do you continue to thank for it or do you drink the water? Having faith that the person is getting you the water, and then receiving it, is how you can enjoy the experience of the water. There is nothing

64

esoteric that needs to be added to Jeshua's words. Ask, believe, and you will receive. The core of the statement is the belief.

Faith is your simple belief. Faith is knowing without seeing. Know that what you ask for you are already going to receive. The simpler your faith the faster you receive. I say simple instead of stronger for one very simple reason, it is easy and not difficult.

Strength implies a struggle. Simple implies an easy relaxed feeling in the body. It is the feeling of the Source flowing through you. The less restriction placed upon the flow the easier the manifestation will be. Once you've asked get out of your way and believe. My friend Holly says, "When you order from a catalog, do you check in with them every day to see if it's coming or do you just know?" This question is an important one for it illustrates the basic simplicity of faith. True faith just is. There is no need for struggle or continued allegiance to a structure or ceremony. It Just is. Know it is and it shall be.

"One reason so few of us achieve what we truly want is that we never direct our focus; we never concentrate our power. Most people dabble their way through life, never deciding to master anything in particular." ~Anthony Robbins

When we realize that the power of creation lies within each of us, as all the Avatars have said, we come to a place of knowing that what we ask for we do receive, then our faith becomes much easier, much simpler.

Chapter 4. Gratitude

What exactly is gratitude?   It is the state of thankfulness we feel when we appreciate the people, things and events in our lives. It is an awareness of what is pleasing to us. New age thinkers teach us that a feeling or state of gratitude is the most powerful avenue to achieving more for which to be thankful. Being thankful means we recognize that in this present moment we have something that is pleasing. Therefore learning how to be grateful now for something that we have not yet seen in our physical reality is the fastest way to manifesting that something. The more you say <u>and feel</u> "thank you" and express your thankfulness, whether to God/Universe or to a person, the closer you are to a wonderful new state of being. And when you get there, and feel thankful for that new state, then you are closer to an even more wonderful state of being. . . and so on. . . and so on. So, what are you grateful for, right now? ~ HM

Thanks

I sit here on my couch and look across at the plant in the corner. A year ago I bought the plant. It was beautiful and lush. I brought it home, repotted it, and placed it in the corner. It began to turn brown. I continued to water it regularly and it began to respond. Over the year I have trimmed away the dead leaves of the past, and continued to water. My intention was to watch it grow and flourish. I was thankful for the plant and in thanks I continued to nurture it, knowing full well that it would respond.

I sit here on my couch and look across at the plant in the corner: five new leaves, each in a different stage of growth look back.

The dead is gone. The plant is healthy. I am thankful for all that I have. I am thankful for all I will have. I know that gratitude is the first step in manifestation. Happy Thanksgiving to all. Keep your eyes on your dreams and be thankful for their existence and know full well they will be achieved.

The Life of Service

"Who is the happiest of men? He who values the merits of others, and in their pleasure takes joy, even as though t'were his own."-- Johann Wolfgang von Goethe

What is a life of service? Many people freely give of themselves in service to others, and truly are the definition of heroes. Service, however, is given in many ways. I applaud the soldier who volunteers to go anywhere, at anytime, to defend people he or she doesn't even know. I salute the firemen, police, and medical personnel who devote their lives to the service of others. But service comes in many ways.

I am always moved by the parents of children who come for healings. They devote their lives to the health of their children. They bathe them, diaper them, carry them, lift them, and continually look for ways to better their lives. They are true heroes.

I met a wonderful woman named Carol Briney who dedicates her life to bringing spirituality into prisons. She gives people a pathway of hope, in a place that is generally thought of in the world as a dead end. Her work makes a difference in the world.

I am always amazed by my assistant Holly, who believes so highly in the work we are doing. She volunteers her time and effort to getting the word out there, and tirelessly arranges the healing sessions we perform. Nothing would happen with my work without Holly's input, and I am truly grateful.

Holly spearheaded the forming of a group of women she terms "Johnnie's Angels" who are volunteering to help get our word and healings out even further. They believe in the work, and are being of service to the cause. They have already started a momentum that is palpable.

To discuss a life of service, we must discuss all aspects of service. Couples, in committing to each other, dedicate themselves to a life of service as well. It is a simple service of remembering and caring about what is important to our loved ones. It is a simple service to remember important dates, anniversaries, birthdays, other important moments. It is a service to remember and express your love through the thinking of their needs, and desires, along with your own. Commitment is a dedication to service. To serve your mate is to serve yourself, and to serve mankind.

No matter what level of service you give, it is always based in love first. Each level is equally important because each level gives love. Because the Source of all that is, is Love, then each expression of Love alters the world on some level. Your service does not have to be devoting all your time and resources. It can be as simple as a smile to someone in need of a smile, or you can express your love by doing a little bit more for the one you love. Each is as important as the one before.

I devoted my life to the spreading of the spiritual message, and to do healings, many of which you can read about in the testimonials. I am always honored by the love I receive from the work. But I also devote my life to the raising of my son, and now, to the loving relationship I am currently enjoying and plan on enjoying for a long time. I know that I will give service in all areas of my life, and in turn, each of these areas will serve me as well.

In what areas of your life do you give service? Can you find other areas in which you could? What difference would it make to others' lives? What would it do for your life? I am joyful.

I thank you God/Universe for all I have.

Gratitude

When I look back upon my life, there are things that were painful, things that were joyful, and things that just were. Each of these moments makes up the life I am living now. Each was a product of my creation with God. I can look back and focus on the painful events and look for the positive result in them. Sometimes we ask for something and the only way we can get it is by having a negative experience so that we may arrive at the moment of our creating. We can look back and focus on the joyful moments and be grateful for the experiences. I look back at look at the results.

I have seen many amazing things in my life. I followed my heart from the beginning. When my family thought I should be starting a 9 to 5 career, I went on the road as a renaissance festival performer. I traveled all over the United States and eventually twenty seven countries. I have seen apparitions and miracles performed. I have seen and experienced pure love emotionally and physically. I have looked into my child's eyes and seen everything. I am grateful for many, many things. Most of all I am grateful for the experiences, good and bad, as I am the one who created each, and each has brought me to a new understanding of myself. Each has been a blessing in the end.

Look back upon your life, remember where you were focused at the time and see the pattern in the creations of your life. Be grateful for each and every event. Be also grateful for the awareness that YOU are creating, and focus on bringing the positive to your life.

A New Way To Start

"We tend to forget that happiness doesn't come as a result of getting something we don't have, but rather of recognizing and appreciating what we do have." -Frederick Keonig

The alarm goes off. The morning is about to burst forward with action towards the rest of your day. Take a minute. Lie there. Think of all you have. Are you alive? Are you breathing? Does the bed feel warm and comfortable? If you have a spouse, are they there? Appreciate where you are, and what you are doing. Institute "Morning Appreciation Sessions," discovering the things you appreciate in your life. Do not focus on tasks of the day, or what frustrations you may be creating.

Instead focus on what is great in your world at this moment. Why try to live where you can do nothing? The future is not the place to create your "now". The present moment is the moment to appreciate. The things you currently enjoy should be appreciated. It is, in fact, the very appreciation of these things that will bring more of the same into your life.

I awoke this morning and appreciated everything in my life: good friends, a wonderful son, and a loving relationship topped the list. No less important was a warm bed, health, happiness, a sunny morning, a cup of coffee, my new hat, and the appreciation grew. I began to experience it spreading out, and a smile erupted on my face. Contentment in my current place. Now I am sure that other things that make me feel content will come rushing towards me, because I am appreciating things that make me content.

Start your day with just a minute or two, or maybe, just maybe, be decadent, and go for three whole minutes of appreciating what you do have - and smile. These "Morning Appreciation Sessions" can alter your life dramatically. Oh . . . also, I appreciate you.

"Life is full of beauty. Notice it. Notice the bumble bee, the small child, and the smiling faces. Smell the rain, and feel the wind. Live your life to the fullest potential, and fight for your dreams." --Ashley Smith

Choice

"There is no way to happiness, happiness is the way". - Buddha

Choice. Choice. Choice. Each moment is a choice. Choice. As the clock ticks by, another moment of choice. We each look forward creating our experience. but that experience does not unfold without choice.

The tire goes flat. I drift to the side of the road. Moments before I was driving seventy five miles an hour down the freeway. The world was flying by me as I passed the cars around me. The tire went flat. I cautiously moved to the shoulder. I am grateful that no one was near me when it went. I didn't think of the inconvenience. I thought in gratitude that I was safely on the shoulder. I never cursed.

I got out of the car and looked at the tire. My jack was not with me but my AAA card was. I called. They said they would send someone to help. I was grateful for AAA. The day was in the sixties when it happened. The trees were green and lush. I sat on the grass basking in the sun and eyeing the lovely scenery. It is beautiful.

The tow truck arrives, the driver comes over and is a pleasant joy-filled fellow who makes me smile. He raises the back of my car and puts the tire on for me. I thank him with a joke, a handshake and a piece of green paper with a number on it. He smiles, laughs, and heads away. I spend a few more moments in the grass.

I get into my car. Away I drive, a little slower. Looking at the scenery around me, wondering what it would be like to sit in the grass there. Or there... there.

The scene would have been different with different choices. I chose happiness. Happiness in each moment. The happiness of gratitude. The happiness of experience. The happiness of loving another. The happiness of eyesight. The happiness of being. The flat tire gave me a new appreciation of choices and the world around me that was flying by without my focus.

Love yourself enough to choose love. Love the world around you. Love the people in that world. Love the tire for reminding you of the choices in your life. Why stress? Choose wisely.

"Remember, we are all affecting the world every moment, whether we mean to or not. Our actions and states of mind matter, because we're so deeply interconnected with one another. Working on our own consciousness is the most important thing that we are doing at any moment, and being love is the supreme creative act." -- Ram Dass

On Thanksgiving

I would like to take this moment to express how grateful I am for the multitude of blessings in my life.

I am thankful for:

- My wonderful son Kynan
- Finding my soulmate Kelly
- My good and true friends - too many to list all, but a few deserve mention: Holly, Tim, Randy, Sharon, Anup, Michael, Stephen and Christy and Johnnie's Angels
- The connection to God I am experiencing
- The life of sevice I am embarking upon

- The roof over my head
- The food on my table
- The air that I breathe
- And the life I am living.

Thank You.
Thank You.
Thank You.

On Memorial Day

"Although a soldier by profession, I have never felt any sort of fondness for war, and I have never advocated it, except as a means of peace." ~Ulysses S. Grant

I do not believe in war. I do believe in peace. I do not believe in hate. I believe in love. Tomorrow is a day of memorial. Though I do not believe in war I believe in courage. I believe in self sacrifice. Around the world at this very moment are men and women who selflessly volunteered to go wherever told to defend you and me. Though I may not believe in the wars they fight or the reasons for fighting them, I do acknowledge their service and their bravery in volunteering blindly, in laying down their lives, in protecting freedom and my right to believe what I wish. God love them. God protect them. And God help us create a world where no one needs to protect us from anything. On this Memorial Day let us give respect to those who have passed. More importantly let us remember the ones still with us, still defending us, still in harm's way. Let us do what we can to make a better world for them so they can lay down their arms and relax.

"You find that you have peace of mind and can enjoy yourself, get more sleep, and rest when you know that it was a one hundred percent effort that you gave - win or lose." ~Gordie Howe

Take A Moment

"You must live in the present, launch yourself on every wave, find your eternity in each moment. Fools stand on their island opportunities and look toward another land. There is no other land, there is no other life but this."
~Henry David Thoreau

Yesterday I was flying home from my California and Oregon speaking trip. On the trip I have been reading a book given to me by a dear friend, The Prophet's Way by Thom Hartmann. I have been having some great realizations while reading it, and one very profound experience occurred on the flight back.

In the book there is a part that asks you to put the book down and have a fully present moment. You see, we as humans tend not to be fully present. We look ahead of ourselves at what we are going to do, or worse, what we are "trying" to do. Then there are those times when we are looking behind at what has happened to us in our lives. The book asked me to do something other than live in a different time frame, just for a moment.

I closed my book on the flight from San Jose to Minneapolis. I sat observing where I was. I didn't judge. I just observed. Realizations of my life in the present began to flood in. I was on a plane traveling. I appreciated that I had the ability to do so. I appreciated that I had been placed in a large comfortable seat with plenty of leg room. I was fed, clothed, and alive, enjoying a life of ease in comparison to many others in the world. I was grateful.

Then something happened that rocked my world and brought me to tears. A hand reached out and took mine. I felt a loving presence beside me, and I realized that I had another person in my present moment. In that present moment Kelly felt compelled to hold my hand. I began to realize the depth of love we have for each other, and in my present moment it filled my heart to overflowing. I turned to tell her and almost couldn't as the tears fell from my eyes. I explained what I was doing and how her simple gesture in that moment meant so much to me. She smiled, made a joke, and kissed me. My present moment is so great and I appreciate it all the more. I am truly blessed in my life.

"These days man knows the price of everything, but the value of nothing." ~ Oscar Wilde

Take a moment. Don't do anything. Don't think about your plans or reminisce about the past. Take a moment and be fully in the present. Appreciate all that you have. Realize that you are a lucky one. Obviously you have a computer. Obviously you can read. Obviously you have the time to afford reading this. The place you are must be warm enough for you to not have to focus on warmth. Are you fed? Appreciate the smallest things in life, because in this present moment you are living them. Someone else's present moment may be hungry, cold, sick, dying. Appreciate the smallest things and realize how completely fortunate you are in the now moment. Love, you.

I am grateful that in this present moment I have you to hear these words with your heart. I appreciate that I am able to read and write. I love all of my friends. I love Kelly and Kynan most of all. I appreciate that I with God, and have created an amazing life.

"One today is worth two tomorrows." ~Benjamin Franklin

    thank you
    Thank You
    THANK YOU

Swashbuckling . . . Apostle?!

"Be yourself. Above all, let who you are, what you are, what you believe, shine through every sentence you write, every piece you finish." ~John Jakes

How does a professed spiritual person justify his work as a Fight Director? I don't. I have always loved my job directing and performing stage combat, or, as I call it, dramatic illusions of violence. My current work is much more of a spiritual endeavor - how do they mesh? I find great joy in that work. I believe that the feeling of joy comes from the truest essence of our source. So in doing the work I do, I am truly living my source. What I do is safe and exciting and the people I work with feel empowered and confident in the end. I have seen over the years people with great self doubt overcome it through learning stage combat.

It may seem that these two professions are at odds. It may also seem that to be a fight director you have a thought or a philosophy that is based in violence. I have found this to be almost universally untrue. I have found the most caring and sensitive individuals at the top of the stage and film combat world. Most of them have a spiritual side to them; many of them meditate and most love to laugh.

"Today you are You, that is truer than true. There is no one alive who is Youer than You."~Dr. Seuss

I feel that in life we need to be true to ourselves. When younger I always had a passion for swords. When the opportunity came to perform a fight I just understood it and had a natural skill. I was offered amazing opportunities by some of the best fight directors in the world and am grateful for their faith in me. They allowed me to overcome many of my self-doubts and embraced me as a brother. I am blessed to have wonderful memories from my life. If it was not for the career I had pursued I would not have been in the places that allowed

76

me to awaken to my truest self. Do I think I will leave fight directing behind? Probably not. I love the work and the brotherhood of the men and women of that field.

What passion did you follow in your life, or did you let it pass by? If so, realize that it is never too late to follow a dream. Let go of your fear and burst forth into the creation of joy that comes from living your dreams. I always wanted to be a fight director. I AM. I always wanted to have my own stage show. I DO. I am living my spiritual life in all capacities. How about you? Do the things that harm no one but make you joyful and you will never fail!

"There are no failures - just experiences and your reactions to them." ~Tom Krause

Happy and Peppy and Bursting with Love

"I find hope in the darkest of days, and focus in the brightest. I do not judge the universe." Dalai Lama

I used to love watching Odd Couple reruns. The dichotomy of the neat freak and the slob was comedy gold. There was one episode where Felix had decided he could write a song and found inspiration in a sports column Oscar was writing, drawing upon the words he was using to describe a violent boxing match between "Berstien and Luftz". Soon the names became, "Bursting with Love." They continued on, all the while Felix finding the positive in each sentence. When Oscar proclaimed his next line to be, "Blood spurted from both nostrils at the sound of the bell," Felix responded, "I can use the Bell!"

"The key to success is to focus our conscious mind on things we desire not things we fear." Brian Tracy

Our world is a mish-mash of various experiences. It falls upon us to see the positive in each. By focusing on the violent or negative aspects, we are truly perpetuating those in our reality. I find that when we look at our surroundings as disappointment, we find more in which to be disappointed. In the Odd Couple, Felix was looking for positive lyrics and because he was focused on finding positive he did. The result of his focus was a complete song. Was it Grammy material? It probably wasn't. But his focus was on creating a positive song.

In truth our lives are like music. Disharmony and Harmony are a choice. Live within the wonderful music of self. Self is the music of your choosing and the music of your soul, and when those two come together you will live the life of your dreams.

"Our thoughts create our reality - where we put our focus is the direction we tend to go." Peter McWilliams

Spiritual Home-Maker

"Love begins at home, and it is not how much we do... but how much love we put in that action." ~Mother Teresa

"Home" - what does it mean? Is it four walls with stuff inside or is it something more? I believe a "Home" is an environment and a "House" is a building. A home can be made anywhere. It takes a very specific type of person to create a loving home. I don't care if you are male or female, the person who is typically at home is the CEO of home affairs and has the most important job of any who reside in that house. The true home-maker has the task of creating the environment that sooths all who reside there. They offer security, love and address issues in a way that creates a feeling of comfort. All of us are home-makers on some level. Some people are responsible for bringing

78

income in to support the house, but the dedicated home maker supports the home.

The many jobs of the home maker never end. The clock is never punched; they just take care of the home. They usually don't take a rest from their duties of home-making and fall asleep with thoughts of how to support the home on their mind. The biggest mistake anyone could make is under-valuing their role. They are the core of the home, the glue that holds it together.

"Nothing can bring a real sense of security into the home except true love."
~Billy Graham

A Spiritual Home-Maker makes an even more harmonious home. Living from spiritual principles, the Spiritual Home-Maker creates an environment of love always. To be truly "spiritual" is to represent the spirit of the divine. Since God is Love, then the divine representation must be loving. Those who stop, take a breath, and think about a loving response when a negative situation confronts them, bring a level of harmony to the home that is visceral. It feels good to be home. It carries an energy of love.

The reason a spirituality inclined Home-Maker has such an effect on the home is that to be truly spiritual is to be aware of your environment. They recognize the environment as a representation of self. A loving state creates a joyful and loving home. "Home," has many aspects: of course there is the house, but there is also the relationships; the décor; the relaxed feeling; the "homey" meals; and the open ear. The belief in home carries the individuals through their day until they once again can rest in the arms of home.

"There is nothing like staying at home for real comfort." ~Jane Austen

Chapter 5. Healing

What is health? Health encompasses so much more than simply the well-being of the physical body. When any process of physical life is off balance, out of alignment, all processes and systems may be thrown off as well. Healing truly encompasses mind, body and spirit. The healing of any of these in turn can heal the rest. True health is the balanced well being of the entire person. People have been healed of mis-alignments and have learned to create health in all aspects with God, many with John Davis's help (read some of the testimonials on www.johnofpeniel.com), and many with others who work with mind, body or spirit. It is in the person's faith in their ability to co-create perfect health, and their willingness to do so, that the miracle of healing occurs. ~ HM

Ask And You Shall Receive. . . Anything

"Whatever you ask in prayer you will receive if you have faith." ~Jeshua

I have a firm belief in a loving God. I do not believe in a judgmental God who desires to be feared. The Apostle John said that "God is Love." It was said that "whatsoever you wish ask in God's name and it is granted." But what is God's name? If we look back to the Old Testament, Moses climbed the mountain and reached the top. On the top he spoke to God in the form of a burning bush. At the end of the conversation Moses asked the bush for the name and God responded, "I AM."

When you declare your state you are directly connecting with God. In stating "I AM sick" or "I AM poor" you are in fact asking in God's name for the state which you declare in his/her name. When you focus on becoming healthy you are in fact declaring that you are sick. Declare that you are healthy and God will grant your request. It was never said, "Ask and if I feel you deserve it I'll give it to you." The thing that brings what you wish is not the declaration, but the faith in the declaration. You have to hold faith that the statement you are declaring is true.

If you are currently sick then declare that you are healed. "Thank you God/ Universe I AM healed." Make that declaration every day with true faith and thank the divine Source for the healing. When you thank someone for getting a glass of water for you, the "thank you" actually completes the transaction on your side. So complete your transaction with God. Have faith in your state of health and you shall receive it. Do not concern yourself with "how." Because when you concern yourself with "how" you are stating that it has not happened and it can't because you are stating that you don't know how. God knows and that is enough. Just put faith in that it is.

"Let it be" ~ Paul McCartney

She Did It

"All the breaks you need in life wait within your imagination, Imagination is the workshop of your mind, capable of turning mind energy into accomplishment." ~Napoleon Hill

She climbed the flight and a half of stairs with the help of a friend and two canes. It was a long struggle to do it. She reached the top. We talked about faith. Did she believe that God/Universe could heal her? Did she have faith it could happen in that room? After a short talk assuring me that her faith was strong, I took her hands and opened to God. I felt the loving wash of Source come through my body . . . she stood. She walked ten feet forward. I asked if she wanted to see something cool. She said yes. "Look where your canes are," I motioned. She turned and saw them ten feet away. She cried. She walked the fifteen feet from there to the stairs. I asked how she felt. "Like I can fly," she responded. She walked down the stairs, one foot in front of the other. At the bottom the people applauded. My friend Holly retrieved the canes for her from upstairs. The joy on her face is why I do what I do.

"In my dreams I am not crippled. In my dreams, I dance." ~Louise Brooks

He Said "I Am" While He Was.

"It is in your moments of decision that your destiny is shaped." ~Tony Robbins

A few weeks ago while doing a healing day at a local Holistic Center, a mother came in carrying her eleven year old son on her back. He had been paralyzed two years before. She set him on the couch in the room where I was working. "Do you believe in God?" I asked him. "Yes," he replied. "Do you believe God can heal you?" "Yes" he replied. "Do you believe God can heal you in this room?" I responded. "Yes" he replied. "Do you believe that God can heal you now?" I strongly responded. After a short pause he responded confidently "Yes."

I stood up in front of him, offered my hands, which he took. He then leaned forward, got his body over his legs and pushed himself into a standing position. After a short time his legs collapsed under him and I set him back on the couch. "Who did that?' I asked. "I did," he replied. I said "Do you want to do it again?" Without delay he said yes. Again he leaned forward got his body over his legs and pushed himself up. While he stood there I leaned down and looked into his eyes, "Who is doing that?" I asked. "I Am" he responded. Soon after, his legs collapsed again. Now his legs were tired so I asked him to lift his legs off the ground and he did. His legs then spasmed and I asked him to relax them out of the spasm and he did. We did that several times, then just the right leg and then the left.

This eleven year old boy was able to make the jump into his divinity. He was creating in time. He touched his inner Christ, his inner Buddha, his inner Krishna, his inner Avatar. He did so in the name of both God and the divine present moment. I am blessed to have witnessed his divinity.

"Once you make a decision, the universe conspires to make it happen."
~Ralph Waldo Emerson

The Secrets Of The Healer

"Every human being is the author of his own health or disease. ~Buddha

I am frequently asked how I heal. Usually I respond "I don't." I have witnessed many healings in the years doing this work and am always awed by the stories of healing. You see, the big secret that everyone looks for is as simple as faith. My task as a healer is not to heal anyone, but to open myself as a conduit for Love to flow through me. When my past life regressionist asked "How do we heal?" the answer was simple: "Create within yourself the remembrance of Love and be it."

The biggest secret is that the healer is very aware that he is not the healer. The healer's job is to find unconditional Love within and hold that space. The feeling of unconditional love is the feeling of the body in a perfect state, in vibrant health. As the healer stands there and emits the love from within, those in proximity feel better. Who wouldn't feel better if they were bathed in unconditional love?

"It is your faith that heals you."-- Jeshua

Then the real healing happens. The person asking for the healing feels well in the present moment and they believe they are healed. By shifting their faith from dis-ease to health, from fear to love, they put faith in the healing. Now I have seen healings at a distance and healings where not a word was spoken. I will tell you that unconditional love supersedes all communication and distance.

Everyone has the ability to be a healer. No one on earth is more or less special than anyone else. We are the Avatars, every one of us. All anyone must do is love unconditionally feel what it feels like, and be it. What does it feel like? Relaxed. It is completely relaxed and joyful. If you are in a positive state you are there. If you experience it then it will swell. If it swells it will heal, but only with faith.

Realize at this moment you are loved. I write this because you <u>are</u> loved. All of these blogs are because you are loved. You are the representation of God on Earth. Each one of you is divine. Each one of you is an Avatar.

"Man is made by his belief. As he believes, so he is."-- Bhagavad Gita

The Physical

"Inward calm cannot be maintained unless physical strength is constantly and intelligently replenished." --Buddha

How's your health? We come here to experience the separation from Source. But the fact that we do come here means we must live physically as well as spiritually. I tend to be a workaholic. I want to reach as many people as possible, and so I tend to work long hours searching for new ways to reach the masses. I do healing days, and go long hours open to Source, allowing my body to be used as a doorway for healing. People often ask me if it wears me out doing the work. In truth, I typically am overcharged at the end of a day of healing, and find myself bouncing of the walls with energy, kind of like a sugar high. If you don't get that reference ask any parent, and they will explain.

After a sugar high there is a definite crash. The same is true for me. When I get charged up, a few hours later I am usually a lump on my couch, zoned out. After weeks of the healing days and late nights looking for work or writing, I begin a phase of lethargy. That is when I know I have pushed my physical body too far, and consciously find things that allow me to not be so strained.

We each are on a quest for our personal truths. Each of our quests can seem so big that we can't or don't want to step away. The interesting thing is that in also taking care of the physical self, you are indeed loving your spirit, and in loving yourself, you are performing a spiritual act. We must live in the physical experience to acquire our truths. We must find the way to the spiritual. In honoring the physical and integrating it with the spiritual, you are being truly spiritual.

When you find yourself eating junk, do you feel good about it? When you've sat on a couch for three days doing nothing, do you feel energized? The feeling inside is the spiritual connection to the body, and this feeling is telling you that you are not honoring the "Temple." When we relax, we feel great. When we laugh and enjoy our time with good friends, we feel charged. A full night's rest with nothing to jump out of bed for in the morning always feels rejuvenating. Give your spirit those gifts and your spirit will gift you in return with more spiritual experiences.

You are a physical and spiritual being. Honor both, and receive the enlightenment you so richly deserve.

"A good laugh and a long sleep are the best cures in the doctor's book".
~Irish Proverb

The Magic Pill

"In seeking ye shall find yourselves and then shall ye know God.~ Jeshua

I love people. I always have. Sometimes the most loving thing you can do is allow someone to make their own path, be that path fun or painful. I have struggled with the desire to heal the world. Sometimes, you encounter people along the path who, no matter how many times they hear the message, will not make change in their lives. Even when the message comes from numerous sources they will not look within. Instead of hearing the truth of the messages they criticize them because they will not consider that the responsibility is their own.

"Know thyself." ~Socrates

My goal in life is to awaken as many people as possible to the power within. It is the choice of each person to either move forward empowered, or to live powerless lives. Many times people will choose the latter. They will listen and hear, but never embody the teachings, choosing instead depression and sadness over a truly joyful life. It is their choice. Each of us must not become invested in the choices others make. Love them unconditionally, but do not take the wheel of their lives for them. It is their experience. If someone breaks their leg and is on a crutch, eventually they have to put the crutch down and work the leg so it will get stronger.

"The kingdom of heaven is within thee. Only when thou hast established the kingdom within and overcome the demons of doubt and fear wilt thou discern the key to the establishment of the Kingdom of God of the earth." ~ Jeshua

86

When one chooses to not take responsibility for their lives and instead looks for the next magic pill, a magic pill will appear before them and they will feel like they have found their cure. When the euphoria wears off and they decide it didn't work, they will look for another magic pill. The secret is that there IS a magic pill, but it might be difficult for some to hear. The magic pill is confronting your fears and making positive change. If an aspect of your life is negative then feed it positivity. See a positive outcome. Act as if the positive outcome is already in your hands. Hold the belief until you witness it in your experience, then live it joyfully. You must first confront your fears. That can be a daunting task. To confront anything negative in life is to have to take some responsibility for it. If Buddha was right and, "what we think we become," then all the responsibility rests solely on our shoulders. All the teachers of old said it was the mastery of self that leads to enlightenment. <u>You</u> are your magic pill.

"Your task is not to seek for love, but merely to seek and find all the barriers within yourself that you have built against. "~ Rumi

The most loving thing I can do for those who are seeking the next magic pill, is to not be it. I cannot be the crutch for those seeking outside of themselves when everything the teachers of old said was to look within. So I will love them and continue to tell them that the power is within until they either listen, or they find fault, and seek the next magic pill. God bless them and I pray they find the way home again.

"A man is as unhappy as he has convinced himself he is." ~Seneca

Intention

"All that counts in life is intention." ~Andrea Bocelli

Intention is the starting action of creation. We must make a decision and intend on creating the outcome. The point of decision launches us into intention. If we keep our intentions aligned with our highest ideals we can achieve great things in our lives. When we focus our intention with the desire to do fearful acts then fearful outcomes are created for our experience. Intention is conscious creation. In our lives we dream about outcomes, but until we intend to do them and take action towards the goal, the outcomes will never be realized. Look closely at your desires. Do those desires benefit you alone? Does your intention make you feel joyful or proud? Will that intention make friends or enemies? Do you desire to do something harmful or hurtful to another? Probably not.

"It is not good enough for things to be planned - they still have to be done; for the intention to become a reality, energy has to be launched into operation."~ Walt Kelly

Inherently people want to be good. It is their life experiences that make them have subconscious beliefs that make them think selfish thoughts. These people are the ones with ill-conceived intentions. The root of their intention comes from a place of dis-ease, and thus is ill-conceived. Fearful thought is the root of all dis-ease. I have witnessed miraculous healings. Each of these healings began with the person intending to see a "healer." That intention was the beginning of their healing. Upon seeing me they had the intention of being healed. Together we brought that intention to a belief of fulfillment in the present moment. That faith in health was the healing fulfilled. It all started with intention. Sometimes we need to break our journey into smaller trips so it seems less daunting. Choose your dream without limitation, then intend on achieving it. Then take the inspired actions towards the goal. Sometimes the action will involve others, sometimes not. It will always involve you. It has to be you, to decide, to intend, to believe, and to receive.

"A good intention clothes itself with power" ~*Ralph Waldo Emerson*

Chapter 6. Relationships

The first context we associate with the word "relationship" in American culture is often romantic encounters. However the dictionary definition is "a connection, an association, or an involvement." This means that we have relationships with all sorts of people, situations and things. It is these connections which give our lives meaning as the social creatures humans are. As we have been learning in John's words, everything in life is on the scale of Love versus Fear, and this applies just as strongly to the relationships we have with the people who cross our paths. Just as we can create unconsciously or with full awareness, so can we create loving or fearful relationships, unconsciously or with full awareness. Although our friends and loved ones have free will to create as they choose, the energy we give out will influence theirs in turn, and will come back to us in the same way. Shine the love you wish to experience! ~ HM

Walking Together

"It is not a lack of love, but a lack of friendship that makes unhappy marriages." -Friedrich Nietzsche

In my work as a healer, I work closely with couples. I find it interesting that the couples' healings are riddled with "she needs to" and "he has to" statements. The healthiest relationships are ones based on one simple fact. The fact is that two healthy individuals come together and choose to walk side by side through life. Each enhances the other's life, and actively thinks of the other's experience, and how they can help.

The second their thoughts turn towards expectation, or projection of what the other should do, then the troubles begin. True friendships are strained when the friend either treats, or is treated as anything but a friend. True and loving friendships have no expectation or projection - they just are. I have a couple of friends that I have had since childhood, Tim and Beau. Each of these men has been such a powerful part of my life, and I love them both as brothers. There are long periods of time when we do not see each other, and yet when we come together again, the conversations start as if it were the next sentence in the paragraph. There is no time of hurt feelings between us.

When choosing to walk together as husband and wife, business partners, or even friends you must release the conditions, and love them unconditionally. Accept them for who they are, and decide to walk together with them in a relationship.

In a marital relationship, friendship is imperative. Love unconditionally, and then express your choice of loving yourself. Be your own friend by letting go of your ego, setting down your walls and barriers of fear, and allow the other to see you for who you really are. Once they do, they also have the free will of choosing to walk beside you.

If you want a loving relationship in your life, then be the loving relationship you want with the one that matters most. If you're not in a relationship currently, then be the relationship, and it will be attracted. Ask for it and then be it.

Co-dependency is a weak foundation to build a successful relationship upon. It only weakens the one who carries the majority of the load. Choose to walk together enhancing your partner, and you will create the relationships of your dreams.

Moving On

"One's first love is always perfect until one meets one's second love" -
Elizabeth Aston

"The love of my life" was what I called Jennifer. For nineteen years we dated, broke up, dated, got married, had a magnificent child and divorced. After the divorce I decided to dedicate myself to my spiritual work. I even chose to become celibate in the process, all the while telling people that Jennifer was "the love of my life." A year after the divorce I began looking at my life and I realized that part of my life was done. I had moved on to a new life without Jennifer. My life was shifting in miraculous ways.

One of the things that allowed me to move on with my life was the conscious shift that Jennifer was "the love of that part of my life." The realization that part of my life was done and I was on to a new part of my life allowed things to flow freely into my life.

In all the healing work that I do, this one tool is given out more than often. Each of the people to which it was given was so invested in the past relationship that they couldn't move forward into something as good or better. When you say the words "the love of my life" about an ex, you are actually saying to God that there is no one as good or better for you, and that was the one love for your entire life. God whose promise was "ask and you shall receive," lovingly gives you no more loving relationships because that is what you are asking for.

Understand that you are the creator of your experience. If you want a loving relationship in your life, then you have to drop the anchors of the past and sail forward into the brighter sunset. As for myself I began to assess where I was in the grand scheme of my life and noticed something missing. So I asked God for a loving relationship and three weeks later it seems to have appeared. Is she the love of the next part of my life? Who knows? What I do know is she is the love of this part of my life and I am going to love and nurture this relationship in the present moment. It feels right.

Relationships can leave painful marks upon us or they can be the most wonderful experiences in the world. They must be fostered, tended and cared for in order to succeed. When they do not succeed for whatever reason, it is we ourselves that have to let them go and move on. I think it is great to remember the person and relationship fondly. It was obviously a wonderful piece of that part of your life. What are you creating for this part of your life? It is OK to move on. Focus on what you want in a truly loving relationship and ask for that in your next. Have fun creating the relationship of your dreams.

People And Stuff

I am finding as I walk down the path of my life that each person I meet tends to have the next stepping stone to my destination. Each person is from God with a message or help for each of us. Once they have fulfilled their mission with us, the relationship can turn stagnant or even negative. God bless them. Always love them for their help. Always be a friend. Know that it is OK to see the situation as a moving on point. Continue down the path, stay present and move forward. No bridge has to be burned, but nothing says you have to walk across that bridge. If you are not in motion, you grow stagnant. I am in motion and am thankful for it.

"One way to keep momentum going is to have constantly greater goals."
~Michael Korda

The Dilemma of "The Fixer"

"Adopting the right attitude can convert a negative stress into a positive one." —Dr. Hans Selve

In life, there are people who are fixers. These people are loving, caring, and genuinely trying to make the world a better place. If, in their personal relationships, they are involved with a partner who has self doubt or self worth issues, the mere act of trying to "fix" can create an undercurrent of fear based negativity. As well intentioned as their suggestions may be, they are not looking at it from their partner's point of view. Those suggestions will be viewed as criticisms and thus, continue to fuel the self doubt.

The shift that "the fixer" must make in this situation is to alter their personal method of fixing. The method needs to shift from an internal perspective to an external one, and more specifically, the perspective of the partner. If the fixer can approach the issue from the perspective of the partner, then they would realize any words that were used could remotely imply fault in the mind of the partner and will create a negative response.

"Dwelling on the negative simply contributes to its power." --Shirley Maclaine

Each person wants love in their life in some form. For some it is simple respect. For others it is full blown Romeo and Juliet type love. Each is a representation of a positive experience. When one has self doubt or self worth issues, any contrary statement to their way of thinking or living is deemed as a criticism, making them feel bad and negative. This negative response creates a negative reaction. When the fixer encounters a negative reaction, they are wired to fix it, thus creating a cycle of negativity that is leading to a negative relationship.

Each person actually wants the same result. It is the pathway to this end result that confuses the situation.

In your relationship are you a fixer? If so, has it helped or hindered your relationship? If the latter, then try looking at your partner's point of view, and give them the love they are actually seeking. Each one of us wants an unconditional love experience. We want to be loved for who we are. We want to know that we are good and lovable people. Find what will make your partner feel loved. Give them that love, and you will see the negativity dissipate. Your partner is dealing with the fear of not being loved. If you give them the love they are seeking, the fear is negated and replaced with love.

Our Best Friends

"It's difficult to understand why people don't realize that pets are gifts to mankind." ~Linda Blair

In life we meet friends who are representative of an unconditional love not felt with others. We term these people our "best" friends, because they make us feel loved, relaxed, amused. I had one such friend - his name, believe it or not, was Odin. Odin was my friend through family strife, relationship break ups, financial issues, but also there for parties, new girlfriends, and joyful reunions. Throughout these times Odin was always there with unconditional love, friendship, and a good lick upon the face. Odin was my Rottweiler.

Animals in our lives are many things: support, love, safety, security, and more. But each is a representation of unconditional love. On rare occasions someone will bring a pet to a healing day. I learn so much every time I work with them. The interesting thing about working with animals is they too have interesting stories to tell. A couple of friends brought an energetic dog with a hip problem into the healing room. The dog ran about the room with a pronounced limp until he stopped in front of me. I reached out and rested my hand on the hip in question. The dog's breathing slowed, and he got instantly calm. After passing some loving energy through my body I removed my hand, and the dog began running around the room.

What I found interesting about this healing was that the dog understood the healing as it happened. He stopped in front of me, and as I laid my hands on him he fell into stillness while the work was happening. He was an active part of the healing, and had a great result.

Sometimes the outcome is a little different. One person brought their sick dog in for a healing, and the owner was despondent over the fact that the dog was dying. I laid hands on the dog, and had an instant knowing that the dog was not going to survive. The owner, who was dependent on love of the dog, had actually reached a state of wanting to commit harmful acts to herself if the dog passed. Now, I do not think of myself in any way as an animal communicator, but I was getting information that this dog was going to come back as a puppy for the owner, and that she shouldn't do what she was contemplating, or he would be alone. So the dog was there for the healing of the owner.

Another interesting story is of a woman who brought her puppy in for a healing. The dog had a very spastic nature and bounced all over the couch and the owners lap. She spastically tried to calm the dog. I looked at the dog and opened to the calm loving Source within. I focused on passing it to the dog. The dog calmed down instantly. I began to talk with the owner telling her that her dog was representing what the dog was getting. Over the next twenty minutes I continually let the dog get spastic with the owner, and then calm with me,

96

expressing to her that the dog was matching her energy, and all she had to do was relax and the dog would as well.

In India there was a young guru named Swaminarayan. During his famed 12,000 kilometer trek around India at age eleven, he wandered into a village that had been the site of nightly attacks by a man eating lion. Swaminarayan arrived in the village at dusk as the villagers were retiring for the evening in their homes as to not be outside during the night hours when the lion attacked. Seeing the young boy coming into the village the people offered him homes to stay in for the night. He refused. In the morning when the villagers opened their homes they were amazed to see Swaminarayan sitting in the square with the lion resting in front of him. When asked how this could be the swami said that he showed the lion no fear, and so the lion gave him nothing to be fearful of.

"Animals are such agreeable friends - they ask no questions, they pass no criticisms."-- George Eliot

What Can You Do For The Love In YOUR Life?

"If you want to be loved, be lovable." ~Ovid

I have recently worked with several couples who have fallen into a fear-based complacency in their spousal relationships. When we find ourselves dissatisfied in our relationships, each of us tends to act dissatisfied with our partner. They in turn mirror dissatisfaction to us. It becomes a downward spiral of negativity. When someone focuses on the negative, God/Universe will give them more negativity because that is the focus. In Star Wars Episode One, Liam Neeson says a very profound line, "Your focus determines your reality."

Everyone wants love in their life. Love, a positive place that is relaxed and easy, needs to be the focus of our reality. If you are in a relationship that is stagnant, then realize that you are creating stagnation. It doesn't matter who started the stagnation. It only matters that you end it. How does one end a cycle of stagnation? Love them first. The reality is that in some form the complacent stagnation is just each person wanting love. Each has been shut down and afraid of doing something that will have them lose the Love in their life.

What can you do for the love in *your* life? Be the love you want. Let your partner experience what it is you seek. That way they can be the mirror of the universe that mirrors that love back to you. Go to them and let them know that you will love them no matter what, that your love is unconditional. There is no condition in which you will not love them. Since they are in the place of fear of not having love, you are defeating the fear by giving exactly what they were afraid of not having.

This is not to say that you shouldn't go your separate ways. This is to say that anything can be changed. The most fearful people in the world are controlling, verbally and physically abusive, and egotistical. They can fall into the trap of addiction or suicidal tendencies. Sometimes it is better for all involved to go separate ways. But complacency is not these extreme conditions and even these can be altered.

To break the chain of complacency is to step out of your comfort zone. One of my dear friends and an incredible motivational speaker, Dan Thurmon, (www.danthurmon.com) says that to remain in motion you must be "off balance on purpose." Falling out of balance creates forward motion. Do you want to stay where you are or do you want to step into motion towards the joyful, fulfilling relationship you want and deserve?

What is the BEST thing you can do for the LOVE in YOUR life? Be love.

Remember you are the creator of your experience.

"If you judge people, you have no time to love them." ~Mother Teresa

Projection

"Before the throne of the Almighty, man will be judged not by his acts but by his intentions. For God alone reads our hearts." ~Mohandas Gandhi

When people walk in fear they look for fear in all things. That being said, relationships can get strained in the process. The most inane comments can be turned into attacks out of fear-based defensiveness. To justify the defensiveness of fear, reasons are projected for it. To need defense is to be in a place of fear of attack. When no attack exists, it is created in the mind to justify the fear. "Please don't turn the TV down," a simple request with nothing behind it, becomes an attack for the one who is projecting. "I don't like your tone" starts the fear based response. "What tone?" eggs the reaction further. The escalation climbs until the fear based anger is in full bloom in both parties. Fear wins.

Have you ever been shocked to find out that you've been mad at someone for weeks? I recently had the experience where I was informed that I have been mad at someone for weeks. The information came after a defensive response to an inane statement. I was shocked! Then I was angered by the hurtful response. It was hurtful, fearful, and baseless. I say it was baseless as it was based on a projection that was not there in reality. I didn't understand, but I realized that the response only fueled the fire of fear, which made the justifications a reality. I quickly apologized for my part as I also gave a fear based response. I am sorry for the fall into fear that I was pulled into. Like in meditation when the mind gets distracted, I will go back to the walk of love and understand that love is the only answer. Thank you for the reminder.

Chapter 7. Love

As you have read, we have been given the gift of fear to better understand the gift of love. Love is the foundation of all creation, so much more than the interpersonal love we think of. Love encompasses gratitude, joy, appreciation, affection, bliss. The concept is the basis of all major religions. I believe that the greatest love of all is the love of self, for when you recognize that love, you recognize your own divinity, your own light, and that awareness of self allows your beautiful light to shine out to others. And then their awareness of their own self-love shines out into the world to others, and thus a web of love light is created. ~HM

Avatars
[Written at Christmas time]

Each religion has its Avatars, Prophets or Messiahs. Each of these magnificent beings brought great truth to the world. Each was right. You see, they each taught love. All of them taught through the various filters of their culture and time in history.

This day we celebrate the birth of one such Avatar. Jeshua Ben Joseph was an enlightened being who spoke of unconditional love of all mankind. His message lives on this day because it is truth. "Love one another" is what he asked of us.

"Hatred does not cease by hatred, but only by love; this is the eternal rule" is what the Buddha tells us.

"Kindness is a mark of faith, and whoever is not kind has no faith" is what the prophet Mohammed taught.

Hindu Swami Vivekananda teaches "To devote your life to the good of all."

This year to come I pray we all find our way past the polarizing thoughts that plague our societies and separate us from each other. I pray that the words of our Avatars fly above the thoughts of fundamentalist thinking and bring us a new dawn of Love.

Dogma

"I think the new spirituality will be a spirituality that's not based on a particular dogma. And that steps away from the old spiritual paradigm that we have created on this planet, which comes from a thought that there is such a thing as being better." ~Neale Donald Walsch

Our societies have been molded by adherence to religious beliefs, ceremonies and dogmas. As we come to an age where we have the opportunity to set aside many of the limitations of our structures, those who fear change will no doubt rebel. Thus we have the hypocrisy of fundamentalists who kill to stop the killing through abortion, and equally the individuals who strap bombs to themselves and walk into crowded markets. I believe some of the villains in the devastation caused by such acts are the various dogmas of religions.

Jeshua said, "The Kingdom of God is within you". That being said, the outer ceremonies and rituals are unnecessary. I was recently invited to be involved in a large scale event know as the "Dance of Oneness". As I delve deeper into the event I realize that many of the "New Age" groups are just creating a whole new set of rituals, ceremonies and dogma. It is the enlightenment of the masses that will bring the kingdom of heaven here to earth, but it is not through standing in some form of geometric ceremony that will do it.

If in fact "God is love," then the pathway to God is through the words of the Avatars of the past. The one who summed it up best, I believe, was Jeshua when he commanded us to "love one another". The pathway to God is through the very act of being love. Embody it, feel it, give it freely, enjoy the feeling of it and realize that it IS God. We do not need more dogma as many of the New Age groups are creating. If anything we need less. Love is beautiful.

"This is my simple religion. There is no need for temples; no need for complicated philosophy. Our own brain, our own heart is our temple; the philosophy is kindness." ~ the Dalai Lama

Love Is Never Wrong

"I always say that as a Christian I cannot find any passage in the Gospels in which Jesus condemned homosexuality." ~Troy Perry

As I have said on numerous occasions I believe fully that God is Love. It is written in the Book of John. That being said I also believe that Love is never wrong. I recently was speaking with a minister at a holistic center where I was speaking. He was quite offended that the center had "homosexual paraphernalia." I asked him what the problem was and he responded that it was a sin. I asked him where he got that information. "Sodom and Gomorrah" was his answer. I asked him to elaborate; he couldn't give me a straight answer especially when I expressed that the translation he was using was from the middle ages, over a thousand years after the Bible was written.

The earliest translation of the Old Testament is known as the Septuagint. When translated today the line that has been mis-translated into "bring them out that we may have sex with them" was originally translated as, "bring them out to us that we may be with them." The minister had no argument that the book had been translated numerous times. Translations upon translations upon translations many times from the new translator's perspective. Have you ever played the telephone game?

In my life I have known many homosexual men and women. I have known some really wonderful homosexuals and some really troubled ones as well. I have also known some really wonderful straight people and some really troubled ones as well. We are all the same. We all want the same things. We all want Love. The minister wanted to be right. He wanted to judge. That is where the minister gets his respect. Respect is how he receives love. He also wants love.

Is homosexuality natural or an anomaly? In all honesty I don't care as long as the people involved are loving, not doing hurtful or fearful acts upon another. Love is never wrong. As far as it being a "sin," as I have said before the word "sin," was translated from three different languages. In ancient Hebrew it translates as "guilt." In ancient Aramaic it translates as "failure" and in ancient Greek "to miss the mark." Each of these translations is a perception of fear. Each is based upon the condition that our self worth is in question. Each is the fear of not being loved.

I wonder if that minister read in the Bible "love one another" - it can't be translated any other way.

"Love one another" ~ Jeshua

Moments

"I am always living very good moments." ~Jose Carreras

There are moments when a surprise catches you off guard. The specific surprise I am speaking of was not an unpleasant event, but joyful. Throughout life you meet people who leave a mark, people who are always special to you on a deeper level. Maybe it was because you experienced good times together, or maybe it was some deeper connection, who knows? What I do know is that when these people connect again, they relive the joyful experience.

Late this evening, so late it is actually the morning, I reconnected with someone very dear to me. It was a fun joy-filled conversation that left me feeling giddy. I thank her for reconnecting. It has shown me once again that life is meant to come with a smile and that our connection to Source can be expressed with a simple hello.

I sit here and feel charged up on the bliss of it all. Do you remember the people in your life that made you feel love? It could be family. It could be a past relationship. It could be a really great friend. It doesn't matter what the relationship was. It only matters how it made you feel. Cherish these moments and the people that create them within you. These people vibrate closer to your soul and thus to your Source. Life is meant to be happy and these people represent that to you or you wouldn't have the feelings you do. Feel it and be grateful for the love that you experience at the mere thought of them. That feeling is a connection to something more divine.

Be You

We can never obtain peace in the outer world until we make peace with ourselves.-- Dalai Lama

Think of the universe as a mirror. When we walk falsely through life, pretending to be other than who we are, the universe reflects the falseness we represent. It brings false people to your experience. When you bravely step out of the fears that have created the falseness and begin to live who you truly are the Universe will begin to reflect the things that make you truly joyful.

People search for the perfect mate. Once someone is in view, they put on airs, play games, and generally portray their false self. If they had indeed met the perfect mate, the mate would pass them by because they wouldn't reflect the false person before them. The potential mate would move along and a false person would move into the picture.

One of the bravest things someone can do in today's world is expose who we are. People in creating their lives fearfully suck in their gut, shave their body hair, and generally put on false impressions to woo a mate. Maybe this is why the divorce rate has skyrocketed well over fifty percent. BE you. Be you in all things. If you feel love, express it. If you feel joyful, express it. Be true to your emotions. Learn who you are. You're pretty cool. After your brave step of being you fully, watch the synchronized dance of God surround you with the perfect people and experiences.

His Holiness the Dalai Lama says "The purpose of our lives is to be happy." Are you happy when you are false? Are you happy when you are someone else for somebody? Does joy permeate your life when you are hiding and not expressing the things that make you happy? Relax. Smile. Connect with people and let them see who you truly are. You will find as I have that life becomes easier. Relationships formed are happier. The finances come from the mere act of doing the things you love.

Be you. You're pretty cool.

Kindness

"A kind word can warm three months of winter." --Japanese Proverb

Kindness. Kindness everyday. Kindness everyway. Kindness. I sit in a restaurant with my dear friend Holly. The waitress comes over, very much stressed. Her face looks flushed. Her eyes look red. She is moving at high speed. "I'll be right with you," she barks as she runs by.

"Can I get you something to drink?" she comes back in a blur. "Iced Tea." "Me too," we said and the waitress ran off with a mission. Time passes and the waitress returns. "You folks decide yet?" flies from her mouth. "How are you?" I ask. "What?" she says confused. "How are you?" I say again. She looks over her pad and snaps out of the cloud of stress-filled confusion and catches eye contact. "Fine . . . and you?" she says. I smile and look her in the eye. "Excellent," I say. "You look like you are slammed," I continue. "Yeah it's busy tonight," she offers. "Just say the word and I'll kick 'em all out," I say with a joking force. "I wish you would," she laughs. The rest of our meal and the time in the restaurant the waitress is laughing and joking with us, actually spending her extra few minutes talking with us at the table.

"No act of kindness, no matter how small, is ever wasted".--Aesop

We can get so frustrated in the small things that pile up in our lives that we can forget everything is easier when we are happy. When someone thinks to give a smile and a kindness of recognizing the stresses of others, and to actively connect with them, their frustration ceases and for a time they experience the love of Source.

When you walk through your day actively notice the people around you. When you come across the person who is not having a good experience, rather than judge them as unpleasant think of the stresses they must be under. Understand, and give them an opportunity to release the negativity of stress and fear and have a better day. I hope that someone will do the same for me when I am in a bad mood. How about you?

"Each small act of kindness reverberates across great distances and spans of time, affecting lives unknown to the one whose generous spirit was the source of the good echo, because kindness is passed on and grows each time it is passed, until simple courtesy becomes an act of selfless courage years later and far away." -- Dean Koontz

Character

"Only I can change my life. No one can do it for me."--- Carol Burnett

I am all for giving someone a hand up when they are down. I recently had a friend show me that no matter how much love or healing you give sometimes they are just unwilling to do the things to help themselves. In fact they may be so unwilling to change that they do hurtful or disrespectful things to the very people who are offering help.

I recently was away on a trip. While away my friend, who was down on his luck and recently homeless, was offered my home to stay in while he figured things out. I returned for an overnight stop on the way to yet another trip. I arrived home and my car was not there - he had been using it without permission. I entered my home to find my house a complete wreck with his possessions and mine strewn across the floor. The lack of respect he showed to my home and things was a complete expression of how little he truly cared. That being said I insisted he remove himself and his belongings from my apartment and car.

So was that the loving thing to do? I would have to say yes. Yes, because without consequences of his actions he would never learn. Without a bottom to hit he wouldn't climb out. He obviously is not ready to love himself or others. Even at my maddest in this, I said to him that I wanted to be his friend but he has to fix our friendship, I would not do it. That was an option, a way up again. I will expect him to make a choice.

We each are the Avatars in our lives, each of us creating through thought, word and deed. His deeds created a reality that may not be to his liking. It is, however, the reality he created. The experience of his world is what it is because of his expression - his expression is his character. It is never too late, character is a choice. Choose a new character like an actor putting on makeup. As the new character becomes your own, your world will change as well.

To show character is to show love and respect. Showing love and respect is living up to your word. I offered him a place when he was down. The character he showed was one of not caring and abusing the hand that was helping. Possessions are things. They don't really matter. Love is all that matters. In situations like this one, the love I had to give was to myself and him. After the experience I had to make sure that he would not abuse my love again. I also had to give him the consequences that his lack of character deserved. I will be his friend, but I will set the limits at the height of his character. I hope that he finds his way in life. He won't until he finds that character.

Joy Pandemic

"Grief can take care of itself, but to get the full value of a joy you must have somebody to divide it with." --- Mark Twain

Joy to many may seem illusory. When someone lives and defines himself by the fears in his life, he does not feel the positive states of Love/God/Universe. Joy is a direct expression of the Source. It is the most visceral of all aspects of love. It tingles within us. It simply makes us smile, express, and manifest our reality.

Many times our fears will overpower our joy and halt any forward motion. People fear judgment of others. This predominant fear is one that directly corresponds to the fear of not having Love/God/Universe. People tend to swallow their joy in an attempt to avoid these judgments. In swallowing that joy they actually deny the Source already working within them.

Find the Joy first, hold on to that feeling and express within your mind and with your words the things that make you joyful. Ask God for more of those experiences. Then actively share your joy with someone else. Hold them in your heart, and your smile shows them the joy on your face. It then will erupt upon their faces as well. The smiles will transfer from one person to another starting a joy pandemic.

"Joy is Prayer. Joy is Strength. Joy is Love. Joy is a net of Love by which you can catch souls." --Mother Teresa

What is Spirituality?

spir·it·u·al·i·ty [spir-i-choo-al-i-tee] -- The quality or fact of being spiritual

I was driving to the airport after a lovely week away. Beside me was my girlfriend. Soon she would kiss me goodbye as I got on a plane and flew home. We drove along and the love within me swelled and I reached across and simply touched her side. It was a simple gesture. She reached across and grabbed my hand and held it.

The book of John says that "God is Love." The simple gesture of reaching for my girlfriend was a pure act of love. The feeling inside me swelled until I was compelled to touch her. Acting upon the impulse of a loving feeling is living spiritually. Jeshua said "love one another." By staying ever present and acting from a loving place you are truly living spiritually.

Religion is a re-living of the spiritual acts of Avatars. Their present moment acts were so powerful that people have been celebrating them for thousands of years. Religion re-lives these acts over and over and over, reminding us of how wonderful they were. I wonder if the fact that they are re-living those acts is why they call it a re-ligion.

Spirituality is here and now. Live your life from a loving perspective act upon the loving impulses and reap the benefits of living spiritually. My girlfriend reached across and held my hand. She also acted upon her spirit. Each spiritual act has an effect.

"We can live without religion and meditation, but we cannot survive without human affection." --The Dalai Lama

Good Morning Bodhisattva.

*"A **bodhisattva** is someone who has compassion within himself or herself and who is able to make another person smile or help someone suffer less. Every one of us is capable of this. ~ Thich Nhat Hanh*

In Tibetan Buddhism, a Bodhisattva is anyone who is motivated by compassion and seeks enlightenment not only for him/herself but also for everyone.

Good Morning Bodhisattva. I call you this because no matter where you are on your personal quest, you are somewhere along the Bodhisattva path. Some along the path awaken quickly, finding the heart centered love that truly allows them to experience their divinity and christ consciousness. Others find places along the path that they will not release, and thus they lose the title of Bodhisattva as they stop the quest for enlightenment. The reality is that they are never <u>not</u> Bodhisattva, because in their frustration they still are seeking joy. Joy is enlightenment.

The word "Namaste" is used as a means of acknowledging the Bodhisattva in another. The divine spark within everyone is Bodhisattva, the part of them on the quest for enlightenment. Everyone has it. No one is further along the path. There is no ranking.

As part of the compassion and enlightenment of the Bodhisattva, one must see the divinity in all. One must release the ego of hierarchy. "Love one another" said one of the ultimate examples of Bodhisattva. Be love. Be love in all things. Be love with all people. Recognize the Source of all in the simple actions of love you create in the world. Leave a trail of joy behind you and you are truly the enlightened one. Good morning Bodhisattva.

Live Your Joy

"Don't ask what the world needs. Ask what makes you come alive, and go do it. Because what the world needs is people who have come alive."
~Howard Thurman

The quote above inspired me to write this blog. It is a simple quote and yet it says so much. Many times through life we bang our heads on the walls trying to figure out our way. We seek material possessions to find fulfillment. To fill that desire we seek to find a means of creating monetary security. We become obsessed with the making of it and in doing so we gamble on the very question "What does the world need?" The question is a good one, but it is the perspective that is skewed. Instead of seeking the "means" or as I like to put it the "how," we need not focus on it at all.

In my life I have always been fascinated by metal fabrication. When the Discovery Channel started airing shows about motorcycle builders I was hooked. Now I don't ride a bike and don't really have a lot of interest in riding bikes. I like my transportation in the four wheeled or winged variety. I watched as each of these amazingly talented craftsmen designed and built these mechanical works of art. One of the best builders was a man called Indian Larry. Larry built and designed bikes for decades. Bikes were his passion. He eventually died performing his famous standing on the seat no hands stunt he was famous for. Once while watching a show about Larry a quote of his stuck in my head: "Do what you love and the money will come."

"Do what you love and the money will come." ~ Indian Larry

For Larry the money did come. He was in alignment with what made him come alive and the universe made him wealthy. More importantly, however, was that Larry lived joyfully. As many know I believe that joy is a representation of divine Source, or as Jeshua would put it, "the Kingdom within." The world needs joy. We are bringing the Source of all to our world existence by being joyful and the universe supports our joy by providing the "how" for us. We don't need to know the "means," we just need to know our joy.

For me these blogs are joyful. The book I am writing is joyful. The speaking, the teaching, the healing is joyful and so I trust the universe/God will provide in whatever "how" it chooses. Remember the Bible says "Ask and Ye Shall Receive." Also remember you are the one asking. The receiving is the "how."

"Joy is not in things; it is in us"~Richard Wagner

What can I do for you?

"Only a life lived for others is a life worthwhile." ~Albert Einstein

A life of service is my desire. But what service do I intend on delivering? I have been very fortunate to have miraculous things happen in my life. Over time I became aware that I was the cause of the miracles in my life. This is not because I was different in any way, but because I became aware of the simplicity of creation. Sometimes I still get in my own way and each of these times is a learning experience for me. I feel as if I have learned so much and yet it all seems to be getting simpler. The simple truth of it all is that you are the creator.

So here I come desiring a life of service to humanity. What can I do for you? I desire to show you the simplicity of it all. I desire to awaken you to your divine self. I desire for you to be empowered. I desire you to be the best you that you can be. Most of all, I desire that you be happy. I feel I could give you many things, but as they say, "Give a man a fish and you feed him for a day. Teach him to fish and you feed him for a lifetime."

So I serve. I serve by writing blog posts to make you think and to show the simplicity of what I have learned. I speak so that people may hear the words and so get the teachings. I do private healing sessions to release fear and ailment. I coach to assist in the long term empowerment. I focus on Healing the Earth as a means of connecting our global consciousness towards a divine purpose. I personally meditate to allow divine inspiration to come through for you. I make jokes to make you smile so you will feel your divine self. I lift people up and if they do not stay up, I offer again. I am expressing to you that we are one with all that is and through divine realization of that fact you are served.

I serve for you. I serve for me. I reap as I sow. I am truly blessed that you allow me to serve. What can I do for you?

"I don't know what your destiny will be, but one thing I do know: the only ones among you who will be really happy are those who have sought and found how to serve." ~ Albert Sweitzer

Chapter 8.   God

The name of the "supreme being" has been debated, fought over, written about and whispered for millennia. Having a Judeo-Christian foundation, I have chosen to use "God" as the term for the Creator. In the context of this book, the label does not matter – the concept is the important part. Whether you use the term universal consciousness, Allah, Almighty, Higher Power, Goddess or any other name you choose, the foundation of John's teaching is that a universal energy, a real force, exists. It is the energy with which you co-create, with which you co-exist, and <u>within</u> which you co-exist. This God-energy is not Michelangelo's old man in heaven, nor a vengeful judging dictator who will smite you down, nor a benevolent grandfather, but instead an all-pervasive energy of love. And when we learn how to tap in and live in that love-force, our lives will change forever. I know – mine did! ~ HM

Spiritual Math

A woman in Texas asked me an interesting question. "Can you explain the trinity?" she asked. I began to hear words forming in my head and as usual I just spoke the words I heard: "One Plus One Equals One (1+1=1). There is your consciousness; there is God's consciousness; and there is the combined higher self consciousness." You are the Christ, you are the Buddha, you are Krishna, you are the Mohammed. Each of these individuals said the same as well. Each was here to empower the individual. Living by example, each showed us the path of our potential. Nothing is impossible to the one who believes it to be so. Live life with the faith and knowledge that you are limitless. As the Torah says and Jeshua quotes ,'Ye are Gods."

Interconnectedness

"Do not be misled by what you see around you, or be influenced by what you see. You live in a world which is a playground of illusion, full of false paths, false values and false ideals. But you are not part of that world." ~Sai Baba

Everything in the Universe consists of atoms. According to Einstein there is nothing solid within an atom. Atoms are purely an energy "event." That being said, think about your breathing for a moment. Now realize that the air is made of atoms as are the lungs with which you breathe the air, and the room in which you breathe the air. Anything you see, hear, smell, or touch is constructed of atoms. Everything is nothing but pure energy.

Where do you begin and end? In reality you are the alpha and the omega. You are your consciousness within the energy of the universe. What is the energy? Consider this for a moment: the energy is God. We are truly created "in God's Image." We are connected directly to the Source. We are connected directly with each other, through the energy of Source.

"In the beginning was the word and the word was with God and the word was God." Consider this meaning of the first lines of the Book of John: In the beginning of what you create is the words you speak and the words go to God and God creates your words around you in his image. The word truly is God. When someone does fearful acts they erupt fear in those around them, to give to that person that for which their words have asked. Synchronically people who are in like alignment with that creation are right there to comply, because the fearful act they are erupting to is in alignment with some fearful creation of their own.

We are all connected with each other; as such, we affect the world on the whole. If you could consciously create a joyful loving

116

experience instead of a fearful experience created unconsciously, which would you choose? When you catch yourself in a negative frame of mind you are consciously recognizing a fear response and then you can consciously change your state and thus the state of those around you. The more of us who consciously create a loving joyful experience, we can in effect change the world.

"Infinite love is the only truth. Everything else is illusion." ~David Icke

Your Direct Connection To Source

"If you smile when no one else is around, you really mean it." ~Andy Rooney

I am a firm believer that God/ Universe is Love. Love is the positive state. I also believe that we were given fear as a tool to experience Love fully. That all being said, I one time while watching a fireworks display saw the world go into slow motion. This phenomenon is not uncommon. Many people speak of moments during car accidents when they can see the world go into slow motion. I watched as the fireworks drifted apart from the center explosion and I heard a voice. The voice said, "I come within a smile." I realized that when we are truly happy, joyful, we smile, and behind that smile is a feeling and that feeling has no pain, no fear, no stress. It is completely open and relaxed. It is the Source within us when it is not affected by our personal fears. It is our true and highest self.

There is a moment in meditation when you can literally watch your body breathe itself. In that moment there is a realization - we don't breathe our bodies. If we did we would be focused twenty four hours a day, seven days a week month after month and year after year. When we breathe deep and relax our muscles in the exhale we reach the same state as in a smile. Consciously breathe that good feeling up to your head on your next inhale and feel the same feeling as a smile right there in your deep breath. Most religions mention the breath as divine. In Christianity, after the resurrection, Jeshua in the upper chamber breathed upon his disciples. The Source/God/ Universe is within you, now, in this moment. You are one with it, and all you have to do is breathe or smile to feel your connection to the divine. If you feel negative (sad, mad, etc.) that is your fear. Recognize it as fear and release it. Surround yourself with the positive state and you will be surrounded with more of the same.

"Inhale, and God approaches you. Hold the inhalation, and God remains with you. Exhale, and you approach God. Hold the exhalation, and surrender to God." ~Krishnamacharya

You Are The Avatar

" The Creator has to be experienced beyond the five senses and the only instrument that can experience in this way, for you, is yourself - in the state of thoughtless awareness in which you declare 'I am' and hold it." ~Barry Long

"Greater works than I have done you will do." "It is your faith that heals you." "You are the children of God." Each of these statements from an avatar of the past tells us that we are as he was and is. We each set the limits of our potential, and since we set the limits then we are truly limitless. The Source of all that is - God, Universal Consciousness, mother earth, whatever you call it - creates whatever we ask of it. Our unconscious creations have brought us to where we are at this moment in time.

The Avatar takes the role by stepping into conscious creation with the Source. The "greater works" are your conscious creations that will indeed alter humanity. I use the term "humanity" as a reference to

118

the experience we are living. There is an expression that is used frequently in metaphysical circles: "We are spiritual beings having a human experience." The experience of humanity is an illusion created to experience the separation from the Source. It is the realization of this fact that each Avatar of the past reached to step into the role of Avatar.

The illusion is created in thought, word and deed. It is the rending of separation that allows us to become the Christ, the Buddha, the Krishna, The Mohammed. Each of these enlightened Avatars laid down the illusion that is created through fear as an example for us to follow. In truth you must be "born again." Children are fearless and love unconditionally. In coming to the state of love that we were as children, we are in fact seeing beyond the illusion. Watch an infant's eyes as they gaze around the room and notice when they notice things. Many times in your illusion nothing is there. The child sees far more than any of us.

"What you think, you become." When Buddha spoke those words he followed them with, "You create your world." The mere focus begins a creation. The conscious declaration of achieving your desire is asking of Source. And it is written "ask and you shall receive." Krishna in the Bhagavad Gita says, "When a person is devoted to something with complete faith, I unify his faith in that. Then, when his faith his completely unified, he gains the object of his devotion." Realize that you are creating in this moment. You are on the cutting edge of creation, on the bow of your ship, wheel in hand, on the sea of possibility.

Oneness vs. Traditions

"Pray in your church. For you and I are sons of one religion, and it is the spirit." -Kahlil Gibran

The Source of all that is inspires such devotion that cultures around the globe, in efforts to understand it, have created structures we call religions. They kneel before altars, they pray to the east, they avoid certain foods all in a means of devotion to spirit. On the surface it can seem quite silly. I think that it is beautiful.

These traditions stem back to an earlier time when mystical things were normal conversation. As science learned more about our world, the mystical nature became less real. People began whispering the words like "psychic", or "ghost", or "miracle." The traditions and ceremonies are a bow to the time before, to history. The thing that I find beautiful in the traditions is that each culture tapped into something larger. Each found the connection and tried to explain or find the path.

The fact that all the cultures of humanity found something larger means it must be the same source. It must be one. So every culture is right in that they not only recognize it but actively seek it. I do believe, however, that we are coming to an age when the traditions will be stripped away for a direct connection to Source.

As science continues to explore our world it is now coming to a new realization. The new realization is that the smaller the particles they study or the more experiments they do, they find that there are larger things at work, a Source of all that is, an energy, or as I call it God. The study has exposed a miraculous intricacy of all that is and it all works simply. It is easy. We make it hard. We effect outcomes. We create with thought. We are one with it all.

"When you realize how perfect everything is you will tilt your head back and laugh at the sky"- -Buddha

Redundancy

I recently was sitting with my fiancée Kelly discussing the new book that I am writing [author's note: *The Simple Path*] and how it is different from writing the blogs. She, in a playful way, said that I was redundant in my blogs. "Of course I am," I responded. You see, it's hard not to be a bit redundant when the message is so simple. You come at it from different angles as to reach the next person in their way of learning. If I were to simplify what I teach it would go like this:

1.) You are the creator

2.) See #1

The Source of all that is, God, Goddess, Universe, Supreme Consciousness, whatever title you want to put on him/her/it will give you what you focus on. Every enlightened being told us it was so, but you are the one choosing what is created. If you think you should be punished you will be. If you think you will be sick you will be. No method is better than any other, but ponder the quotes of the Avatars and see how each is expressing your divinity:

'The Kingdom is within" ~ Jeshua

"What we think we become,"~ Buddha

"Even the least among you can do all that I have done, and greater things." ~Jeshua

"Man is made by his belief. As he believes, so he is." ~the Bhagavad Gita

"In seeking ye shall find yourselves and then shall ye know God." ~Jeshua

"Whatever you ask in prayer, you will receive, if you have faith." ~Jeshua

"Whatever mishap may befall you, it is on account of something which you have done." ~the Prophet Mohammed

"Be the change you want to see in the world" ~ Mahatma Gandhi

"An infinite number of galaxies are created, sustained and destroyed; yet, without my permission, not even a single blade of grass can be unearthed." ~Swaminarayan Bhagwan

I think these guys are redundant. Each says the same thing just in a different way. Remember you are the creator. The Universe is yours to do with as you please. It is as simple as staying in the stream of focus that leads to your desires. Hold faith in what you are creating until you hold it in your hand.

Spiritual vs. Material

"What we really want to do is what we are really meant to do. When we do what we are meant to do, money comes to us, doors open for us, we feel useful, and the work we do feels like play to us." ~Julia Cameron

It seems of late that God is asking me to define my relationship with my spirituality as it pertains to money. I had to come to grips with the fact I was also deserving of God's abundance while doing his/her works. It is a tight rope to walk in this world. Most of the world has a belief that spiritual people devote their lives to God and that means to live without means. This concept is a throwback to a much different place and time. India today has many spiritual leaders. Each of these leaders is clothed, fed and housed by benefactors or by their followers. In biblical days, Jeshua was befriended by Matthew, a wealthy tax collector, Lazarus a wealthy landowner, and Joseph of Aramathea, a wealthy landowner who at the end of Jeshua's life paid for his body and placed it in his own tomb. Jeshua was clothed, housed and fed.

Our modern society does not function in the same way. Priests receive salaries. Famous spiritual speakers receive payments. Spiritual readers charge by the hour. I recently found myself once again looking at my debts. From month to month I was never sure if I could pay all the bills. Oh, sure the rent got paid but others sometimes had to wait. I realize as a creator of my own experience that it must be a belief of my own that has caused my struggle with my finances. I began to search within for my blockages. I discovered two things in my search. The first was that I associated spirituality with poverty, and the second was that I didn't think I could control my finances. You see, I was raised in a poverty mentality. My family struggled for money and I was told repeatedly by an unknowing father that I was a "bum" and "worthless." So my belief system was that I couldn't achieve financial success.

"It is not easy for men to rise whose qualities are thwarted by poverty."
~Juvenal

Recently I decided I needed to break free from the bonds of poverty and I put some things out on Facebook. First I decided that the two bedroom apartment I was living in was too small for me, my son, my fiancée, two cats, and an elderly aunt of my fiancée's that we were going to be taking in soon. So I asked for help. I asked in the form of a posting on Facebook. I suggested that if each of my Facebook friends would give me twenty dollars I could raise the down payment for the house we needed. The response was quite interesting.

A couple people were offended that I would even ask. Several people actually helped out and most ignored the posting.

So I asked myself again is it my belief system that led to the response. I concluded it must be, as I am the creator of my own experience as all the Avatars have said. So I also posted a reduced rate for my spiritual phone sessions. The first response was someone asking me why I even charge for them. I responded that I had dedicated my life to spiritual work and that I also needed to cover the material expenses that our society creates. I was supported by several people. I am most proud of my nephew who eloquently came to my rescue.

Then a posting came on my blogpost "John of New~John of Peniel," once again questioning my material gain from spiritual work. I fell to the words I fall to most, "God is Love." If God truly is Love then He/She would never want any of us to suffer poverty. God is the ultimate abundance and the Peniel experience is one of realizing that you are a part of God and He/She works in and through you without limitation. I AM abundant. I AM financially secure. I AM Loved by God and I AM confident that God will provide.

"He had heard people speak contemptuously of money: he wondered if they had ever tried to do without it." ~W. Somerset Maugham

Our world dictates that we must have roofs over our heads, food on our table and clothes upon our backs. The only way to achieve those material items is to have an income. I am blessed in my life to witness miraculous healings, and though I do not take the credit for the healings I have given up a lot of gainful work to facilitate healings. My choice of career is spiritual. My choice in the material world is now financial security. I am blessed to be the creator of that experience and am moving forward in great joyful anticipation and in full faith that

God/Universe will provide in abundant ways, that I may indeed continue my spiritual mission undistracted.

The Little Sage

"Every child comes with the message that God is not yet discouraged of man." ~Rabindranath Tagore

Yesterday morning as I drove my six-year-old to school he asked me to sing the "There Was Old Lady Who Swallowed a Fly" song. If you don't know the song your life is incomplete. In the song she progressively eats something larger to catch the one before. After each is swallowed you sing the whole list. At the end of the song it ends with her dying after eating a horse. Kynan and I have a game we play where we add to the song and keep getting bigger and bigger things. Yesterday we had added: a dump truck, the earth, the galaxy, and the sun, when I declared, "Nothing's bigger than the sun." "Nyah-uh," Kynan responded, "Two things are bigger." When I asked what was bigger he told me the universe and God were bigger. So I asked, "God is bigger than the whole universe?" "Yes, 'cause God told me he is everywhere," he continued. "Is God in my coffee?" I asked. "No" was his reply. "He is in you and everybody and we control the God Part inside of us." So obviously God is within each of us . . . but not in coffee.

"We control the God Part inside us" ~Kynan Davis

God is Hot Water

"God always takes the simplest way. ~ Albert Einstein

Many people have heard me speak about the simplicity of connecting with Source. I am a firm believer that religions are history lessons of other people's spiritual experiences, and that spirituality is in your present moment. I talk about God/Source being Love, and fear is the tool to experience God fully. To put it in another way, your positive moments are experiencing the divine Source and your negative experiences are of your fear. That being said, the simple realization that positive experiences are touching God, can happen pretty regularly in an average person's life.

Knowing my belief on this, my love Kelly recently exclaimed, "God is hot water!" I asked her to explain. "Well if God is your positive experience and I love a hot shower, then God must be hot water." Her answer was perfect. It said so easily how close we are to our connection to Source. The simple enjoyment of hot water made Kelly smile. It felt good. Good is only one letter away from God. Bad only shares a 'D.' The simplest moments of joy in our lives are directly connecting to Source.

My belief is that fear is the tool to experience God fully. If in fact that is the case, then we are here to experience our separation from Source so we can fully understand the feeling of it. Ask yourself this question: Would God make it hard? She/he made it so simple that we overlook it. God is with you every day in the simplest things. For me, God is in waking up and seeing Kelly's smile, in my first cup of coffee (though Kynan may disagree), in writing these blogs. For Kelly, God is hot water. Where in your life do you experience the positive emotion that is God? It is the only present moment you have to do so. Enjoy your life knowing you are never alone, you are always connected to God, and that you are safe.

"Where love is, there God is also." ~Mohandas Gandhi

✳

Oneness

"All differences in this world are of degree, and not of kind, because oneness is the secret of everything." ~Swami Vivekananda

We come into this world to know and experience the Source, God, Universe, whatever your particular label is. I will use God. We come to know God through our experiences. We come to know him/her through our feelings. We come to see him through our senses. We experience her through our own doorway.

God comes to know us through our experiences. She comes to know us through our feelings. He comes to see us through our senses. God experiences us through our own doorway. The source we are seeking is ourselves and God together. The Illusion of the world is a construct of belief that allows us to experience our separation from God so we can experience God fully. The illusion, built of formless energy (atoms), makes up the entirety of our physical experience. Everything we experience comes into our lives through our senses. Our belief is built upon the data of our lives.

"Quantum physics thus reveals a basic oneness of the universe." ~Erwin Schrodinger

The senses are impressions that give us a feeling response. That feeling response is our direct connection to God. If God is Love, as the Bible says, then we must measure our feelings against the feeling of Love. The simple realization that the feeling of pure unconditional Love is God, and that we choose to experience varying degrees of separation to have full understanding of that Love, allows us to realize that we are an active part of God, each one of us. Every person you see throughout your day is another aspect of God experiencing self through separation.

The separation we feel is our fears. The illusion persists even when we are in fear. So If the illusion is always there, then God must always be there. If other people are there, then God must also be there. If you feel anything, then God must also be there. The illusion that surrounds you is one of your beliefs. Your beliefs correspond with others' beliefs, and so our illusions intersect. Stepping back from this idea you realize that we are just one giant entity. The entity includes everything, you, me, the earth, the universe, everything. We are one. And so as you walk through your separation experience, realize that you are not separate. You are one with it all. The representation before you is the illusion of your faith. That faith can be altered and the new illusion will morph into a new illusion. The people around you will move in and out of your experience depending on their shifting faith. It is all divine. God's consciousness, your consciousness, and the combined self as one, is the trinity: Father (God), Son (you), Holy spirit (God/You as one).

Acting as one with everything, seeing the world as a representation of self, allows us to alter the negative aspects and move easily into joyful creation. In finding our oneness we find our way home. I often use the joke, "So nice to meet me" - now you know why.

"From oneness, He has brought forth the countless multitudes. O Nanak, they shall merge into the One once again." ~ Sri Guru Granth Sahib quotes

Afterword

Our age is blessed with an abundance of teachers of New Thought, Law of Attraction and other empowering belief systems – Abraham as channeled by Esther Hicks, Joe Vitale, John Assaraf, Wayne Dyer, the Rev. Dr. Michael Beckwith, and Louise Hay, for example. In the last many years as I have been led to each teacher in turn, their teachings made sense of the ebbs and flows of my life, and gave meaning to the synchronicities. Their work also meshed with my many years of self-exploration and growth with personal teachers. All of this exploration prepared me for the life I now lead – supporting those who also are working to empower and enlighten the planet.

One of these bringers-of-light is John Davis, with whom my work began in a reality-shaking way. We had become acquainted many years ago through my regular attendance at a local renaissance festival, where John had performed for years in the comedy swordfighting act Hack and Slash. A friend mentioned that John had a spiritual side and a website on that topic. Reading the website, I was moved and excited to see ideas that could have been written by me, they so closely echoed my own beliefs and studies. Pleased and interested to see this deeply spiritual and moving side of the comedian I knew, John and I became a sort of email "pen-pals" and in the process became good friends.

Now the amazing part. About seven years ago, while cleaning the hall after an event I had run, I found a tiny silver ring with a beautiful ivy engraving on it and an inscription of a Bible verse on the inside. I tried for months to find the owner to no avail and something told me to keep it safe.

Several years later, in 2006, the week before the renaissance festival was to open I was looking for something in the basket where I had years before placed this ring. My fingers touched that lost ring, and I felt a WHOOSH of electrical energy through my body, as if it were charged. I picked it up and for the first time in all those years noticed the inscription on the inside - John 15:5. I looked up the verse: "I am the vine, you are the branches. He who dwells in me and I in him shall have much success." Totally astounded, I knew without doubt that these words were a message for John, so I e-mailed him to say that I had something to tell him in person. He was intrigued, but after all his amazing spiritual experiences, not surprised, and so we arranged to meet at the festival.

On opening day of the renaissance fair, I was wandering around when John found me, and we went to a relatively quiet area to talk. Shaking with emotion, I pulled out the ring and handed it to him so he could see the inscription. His face went white and he said, "OH my GOD!!" I handed him a small cloth where I'd embroidered the verse so he'd know the reference. He got tears in his eyes and hugged me hard – we were both highly emotional by then! When he calmed a bit, he explained to me that he'd been praying for guidance: Was this the time for him to give up the security of his entertainment profession to do spiritual work full time? Was it time to really step into his mission? And then I showed up with the ring. I cannot express the awe I felt then and still feel when I realize that I was the safe-keeper all those years of this special message meant to support John, held for the time it was intended to be revealed. And in the process, I gained a nickname – Frodo the ring bearer!

Since that special life-changing moment with a ring and a renaissance festival, I have worked with my friend John in many capacities to further the important work of empowering people to live their best lives. We have developed a website with all sorts of resources, we speak and present and do healings all over the country, we write newsletters, we confer on new ideas to develop the work to reach more people. John is a humorous and inspiring writer, and when we discussed how to reach more people with the wonderful blogs from the website, a book seemed the logical solution.

I have been honored to witness so many miracles, healings, synchronicities, blessings . . . and to have been transformed in the process. It is my privilege to have compiled this collection of John's ideas, and it is my greatest wish that the concepts presented here will bless you, teach you, and enlighten you. As John says, YOU are the Avatar, the Creator, the Designer of your life, and through God you can be anything you choose. Choose wisely, my friends.

~ Holly Matson

Notes

Notes

Made in the USA
Charleston, SC
29 March 2011